D. Caroline Coile, Ph.D.

Pekingese

Everything About Purchase, Care,
Nutrition, Behavior, and Training

Filled with Full-color Photographs
Illustrations by Michele Earle-Bridges

BARRON'S

CONTENTS

A "PEKE" INTO THE PAST

*Gaze into the eyes of the Pekingese
and gaze into the distant past,
into a mystical world of emperors
and dragons, of symbolism
and ceremony.*

Of Buddha, Lions, and Dogs

The Pekingese is a living artifact, an unbroken genetic link with the ancient imperial world of the Orient. Its ancestors were royalty in every sense of the word—and the Pekingese is not about to let you forget it.

The story begins long ago in the Far East. In classical times, China traded with Tibet, Rome, and Egypt, and Maltese dogs from Rome were probably introduced to Tibet and China by these traders. The dogs of ancient China included hunting dogs, watch dogs, and larder dogs of the chow chow type, but there were also small, puglike dogs with short muzzles known as ha pa ("under table") dogs, which appear to have been kept as pets by the

DNA research suggests the Pekingese is among the oldest of all current breeds of dog. Today's Pekingese are living artifacts from the past.

wealthier people as early as 700 B.C. The ha pa, possibly with influence from the Maltese, is probably the foundation of the "lion dog," the earliest incarnation of the Pekingese.

Lion Dogs

The Pekingese owes its most revered existence to the spread of the Lamaist form of Buddhism to China from Tibet around 700 A.D. One of the strongest Lamaist symbols of Buddha was the lion, a wild beast tamed by Buddha to become his faithful servant. The lion of Buddha could appear in different-sized forms. One legend tells of how the lion implored Buddha to make it smaller, but to retain its great heart, so that it might court the marmoset it loved so much. Ah Chu, the patron saint of animals, granted the lion's wish, in so doing creating the diminutive lion dog with the size of the marmoset and the great heart and courage of the lion.

Few other breeds can claim the long association with royalty that Pekingese can.

Foo Dogs

Because there were no lions in China, the Foo dogs of the palace (probably a derivative of the *ha pa* dog), which bore a remarkable resemblance to a tiny lion, soon replaced the lion as the exalted symbol of Buddha. The Chinese were masters at creating beauty and art in a variety of ways, including shaping living plants and animals to comply with their sense of aesthetics. The lion dog was perhaps their crowning glory.

Much of the success of the Chinese in breeding these fabulous little lions lay in the unlimited resources available to the emperors who directed their production. Palace eunuchs were in charge of extensive breeding operations. The Tibetan monks also had the resources and time to devote to breeding dogs, and they, too, developed a small temple dog that may have been incorporated into the development of the Chinese lion dog.

Genetic Evidence

DNA research has suggested that the Pekingese may be one of the oldest breeds of dogs.

Life in the Palace

The emperors of the T'ang dynasty (700 A.D. to 1000 A.D.) were especially devoted to the lion dogs and their mystical connotations, and it was during this era that the lion dog was perfected.

As the living symbol of Buddha, the lion dogs of the palace lived lives of splendor and luxury. At the height of their favor they were literally treated as royalty, some even being given royal appointments. The finest dogs were guarded and pampered by their personal servants, fed the choicest foods, and bathed in perfumes. The smallest dogs found special favor as "sleeve dogs," and were carried about in the huge

The lion dog remained an important religious symbol through the Han, T'ang, Sung, and Ming dynasties.

The Pekingese was quick to conquer the Western world.

sleeves of the robes worn by both men and women. Pekingese partook in all ceremonial affairs, bedecked with ribbons and bells, some preceding the emperor and announcing his arrival with short barks, while others trailed behind to carry the train of the emperor's robe. The penalty for taking such an exalted animal from the palace was "death by a thousand cuts." Yet such were the rewards for smuggling that the eunuchs often arranged for dogs to be spirited away, so that these royal dogs eventually found their way into the homes of wealthy Chinese and even Europeans.

Colors: The most popular colors of the dogs within the palace were the fawns and reds, perhaps because they were the most lionlike. All white dogs were greatly prized. Dogs having a white mark in the center of their forehead were also favored, because this mark was said to be one of Buddha's superior marks. Also in favor was a sashlike mark on the body, suggestive of the yellow sash worn by some members of the imperial family.

Decline in Buddhism

Very few breeds can claim so long a period of sustained selective breeding and exaltation as can the lion dog. The lion dog remained an important religious symbol throughout the Han, T'ang, Sung, and Mongul dynasties. Only during the Ming dynasty did the popularity of the lion dog cult wane, accompanied by a decline in Buddhism. Still, the lion dogs remained as pets of the eunuchs and women, albeit without the fanfare once accorded them. And although the eating of dogs was common practice, the lion

Pekingese come in a wide variety of colors.

dogs were never among the breeds included on the menu. When the Ming dynasty was overthrown by the Manchus in the seventeenth century, Buddhism returned to favor and the lion dogs were once again embraced as religious symbols.

Taken to England

Although occasional lion dogs had made their way to Europe, they were not maintained there as a breed, and so had little influence in the Western world until the magnificent Summer Palace was looted by British and other troops in 1860. The emperor and his family fled, apparently taking with them many of the nearly 100 dogs normally in the palace, and leaving orders that the remainder be executed rather than fall into foreign hands. But left behind were five lion dogs belonging to the emperor's aunt, who had taken her own life. The dogs were taken to England, where one (a fawn and white, later named "Lootie") was presented to Queen Victoria, and the others were bred. Most of all, these oriental treasures enchanted everyone who saw them.

The living symbol of Buddha now commands homes around the world.

The Legacy

This was the beginning of the end of imperial China; the last Dowager Empress T'Zu Hsi died in 1908, and was laid to rest amid ceremonies that included models of her favorite lion dog. She left behind a poem describing the lion dog (from which many claim the current official standard was derived) and a legacy of some of the finest dogs the world had ever seen.

The Occidental Tourist

There were still lion dogs in China, but the large-scale breeding within the palaces would never be seen again. The lion dog had become the pet of the common people, having been made available through the disposition of dogs bred in the palace but not considered of high enough quality to keep. Some of the dogs made available in this way at the monthly trading fairs were probably the source for many of the early importations. Others were forcibly taken from pet owners by the occupying troops. Unfortunately, since these dogs did not represent the imperial ideals, they did not form a good genetic basis for the breed in Europe. However, an occasional palace dog was allowed to leave for Europe. Two such dogs were "Ah Cum" and "Mimosa" in 1896, who, along with "Boxer," can be found heading many modern-day pedigrees.

Europe: The first Pekingese sauntered into a show ring in 1893, although only in 1898 were official classes just for Pekingese offered and an official standard agreed upon. The first English champion was Ch. Goodwood Lo.

Disagreement continued over what to call the breed. The Chinese had never called it a "Pekingese," but Europeans dubbed it that after the city in which they had been discovered. Various associations called the dog by different names. The Pekingese Club was formed in 1904, followed by the Pekin Palace Dog Club in 1908. The latter club was formed to encourage the breeding of Pekes that weighed less than 10 pounds (4.5 kg). This had been the original weight limit set by the Pekingese Club, but that club changed it to 18 pounds (8.1 kg) and then removed any weight limit from the standard.

America: The Pekingese was meanwhile arriving in America, often a treasured souvenir of the trips abroad made by the affluent. In 1906 the American Kennel Club officially recognized the Pekingese. The early specialty shows held by the Pekingese Club of America were fabulous social events, attracting not only hundreds of Pekingese, but perhaps the most elite exhibitors ever seen at a dog show. Prices for puppies were spectacularly high and the Pekingese was clearly the breed of high society.

At the Peak

Although these oriental wonders attracted much attention, their small litters kept their numbers down, and many of the breed's early fanciers were not interested in selling their precious stock. The breed could count as its devotees some of the West's most influential businessmen, politicians, and royalty. When the

The crowning glory of royalty, the Peke's coat should form a lionlike mane around the neck and shoulders.

breed finally became available to everyday pet owners and dog fanciers, it began a meteoric rise to the top.

Today, the Pekingese is among the most popular of toy breeds, providing a rare opportunity for commoners to mingle with royalty.

PEKE PERKS

The Pekingese is a product of thousands of generations of selective breeding for imperial demeanor as well as lionlike appearance and beauty. It does not look like other breeds, and it does not act like other breeds, nor should it be expected to.

The Pekingese Personality

The Pekingese still plays the role of royal dog with the same calm dignity that it must have displayed in the emperor's palace. As befitting an object of adulation, the Pekingese is gentle but condescending, and remains aloof with strangers. This is the public Pekingese—haughty, deliberate, regal, and sedate. But the private Pekingese is another animal entirely. Around its family, the Pekingese is apt to change from court royalty to court jester, uncovering a joie de vivre and remarkable sense of humor reserved to share with only a special few.

The Wild Side

The Pekingese has some more surprises in store for those who get to know it. First of all,

Despite appearances, the Pekingese is no sissy lapdog. It is independent, strong-willed, and adventurous—but it may bite off more than it can chew.

contrary to popular belief, this is no "sissy" lapdog. Even extensive selection for royal demeanor could not erase the natural instinct of the Pekingese to, at times, be just a dog. The Peke likes nothing better than a jaunt afield, where it will give chase to a rabbit with a fervor that would make any Beagle blush. It also will not hesitate to plunge into a lake, poke its flat face deep into a hole, or subject its magnificent coat to an occasional mudpack and cocklebur beauty treatment. This stately palace dog has a definite wild side.

Courage: In fact, the Pekingese is a tough character. It will not start a fracas, but it will never back down from one. Its courage is virtually boundless. This courageous attitude, coupled with its calm disposition, makes the Pekingese the ideal watchdog. It does not yap incessantly, or call the alarm to a falling leaf, but when it does bark, its owner can be sure that there is something of which to take note.

Independence: Many dogs are dependent upon their owners, looking to them for guidance at every turn. Not so the Pekingese. It is fiercely independent, and this trait, combined with its indisputably strong will, can be exasperating to the first-time Peke owner. The Pekingese does not have a stubborn streak; it has a stubborn body. When the Pekingese plants its feet and says "*No*," it becomes a canine anchor. Attempts to force it into compliance result in only more determination to have its own way. When it comes to doing nothing, despite all urging to the contrary, the Pekingese is among the unchallenged masters of dogdom.

Intelligence: Pekingese are extremely intelligent dogs but they need intelligent trainers who can mold their training techniques to work with, rather than against, a dog that does not act like most other dogs. Trained correctly, the Pekingese can be an obedient and trustworthy companion; yet it will never be a fawning slave.

Family: As befitting any royalty, the Pekingese does not immediately take to strangers. It is a one-family dog, and does not hesitate to discriminate between family and non-family. Still, with time it will gradually warm up to new acquaintances, and once accepted as friend, it displays undying loyalty

and devotion. Indeed, one of the breed's great charms is that it requires people to earn its friendship, unlike so many breeds that seem all too eager to abandon their family for the first stranger who throws a ball.

The Pekingese loves its family dearly, but it is not overly demonstrative. Apart from an exuberant greeting, it prefers to honor its loved ones with an occasional kiss, never indiscriminately nor insincerely given. Not a lapdog by nature, the Pekingese will nonetheless acquiesce to sitting in your lap if you ask it nicely. Although left to its own it would probably prefer to sit very close by your side as an equal, it will trade a slight loss in dignity for a soft caress.

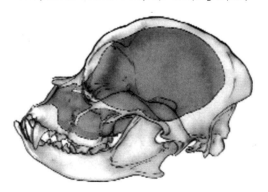

The Pekingese skull. Note the prognathic (undershot) bite and limited nasal area.

If the eyes are the windows to the soul, then the Pekingese has the best view in dogdom.

The Pekingese is indeed royalty, and it will never let you forget it. But it is equally willing to appoint its family as royalty as well, and make its home, no matter how humble, an imperial palace.

Pekingese Predispositions

The very traits that make Pekes so appealing can also make them more prone to some health problems.

Brachycephalic syndrome: Pekingese are brachycephalic, which means they have flat faces with short muzzles. This configuration also means they have compacted respiratory systems, which leads to a condition called brachycephalic syndrome. This condition consists of a group of anatomical abnormalities that may lead to breathing problems ranging from the Peke's snoring through heat and

Carefully bred Pekes are relatively free of health problems, and make the best pets because they have the promise of longer, healthier lives.

Pekes are quiet and charming household companions.

TIP

Prognathicism
This is the term for an underbite, where the bottom teeth protrude farther forward than the top teeth. Undesirable in most breeds, it is the proper and typical jaw conformation for the Pekingese—within limits. Overdone, the tongue may hang out, and chewing may be difficult.

Achondroplastic Dwarf
This refers to a type of dwarfism caused by arrested development of the long bones, without a concomitant reduction in bone diameter. In a sense, the Pekingese is a rather large, heavy dog with short legs. Achondroplastic dwarf breeds tend to have a characteristic bow to their front legs, so that the leg turns in around the pasterns but back out again around the feet. This conformation results in the Pekingese characteristic rolling gait, and also renders it an unlikely Olympic hopeful.

exercise intolerance to life-threatening breathing difficulties. Stenotic nares (abnormally small nostrils), which are often seen in brachycephalic syndrome, decrease the amount of air flow when inhaling; severe cases require surgery to enlarge the nostrils. Another common component of brachycepahic syndrome is an elongated soft palate, which can swell and partially obstruct breathing if the dog pants heavily.

Heat: Pekingese are heat-intolerant. Dogs build up heat according to body mass and give off heat according to body surface. The Peke's heavy body has a minimal amount of body surface compared to body area, and that surface is covered with thick hair, so the body tends to hold heat more than the average dog. Dogs rid themselves of excess heat by evaporation of surfaces of the tongue and respiratory tract. The Peke's face, muzzle, and respiratory tract have relatively little surface area available for cooling. Pekes build up heat and can't shed it, making them at risk of deadly heatstroke in even mild weather. Pekingese owners must be prepared to shield their dogs from overheating. You must be willing to run the air-conditioning even when it's not terribly warm, and be prepared with ice packs in the event electricity fails or a car breaks down.

Pekingese tend to have fairly prominent eyes.

Eye concerns: Pekingese tend to have fairly prominent eyes, which renders the eye surface more susceptible to scratches and drying. In some Pekes, the eyelids do not close tightly, causing the surface to dry so much that vision is lost. In other Pekes, the hair growing from the fold of skin over the nose touches the eye surface, irritating it and leaving it susceptible to infection.

Wrinkle dermatitis: The fold of skin overlying the nose can be a source of another problem. If the wrinkled area is allowed to remain moist, the area can become infected. Peke owners must be diligent about keeping the wrinkle clean and dry.

"The Pekingese is a well-balanced compact dog with heavy front and lighter hindquarters." From the AKC standard.

SEEKING A PEKING DOG

Finding a Pekingese is not difficult, but finding a quality Pekingese is a far greater challenge. Whether you want pet- or show-quality, finding a dog with a good temperament and good health is essential.

Rescue

Responsible owners provide a home for life for their Pekingese, and responsible breeders provide a safety net in case the owners of their puppies can't fulfill that commitment. But not all owners and breeders are responsible, and sometimes unforeseen circumstances prevent good intentions. Pekingese may be lost and never claimed, they may be orphaned by deceased owners, or they may be given up because of health or financial problems.

Rescue Pekingese range from puppies to seniors, but have in common a need for a forever home they can call their own. Occasionally, rescue Pekes have behavior problems, often stemming from poor training or socialization, but good rescue organizations will make sure you know any problems ahead of time and will help you guide your Peke to becoming the

Born to the royal life.

best dog he can be. (See page 92 for contact information on Pekingese rescue groups.)

Good Breeders

The quickest way to find a Pekingese may be through a pet shop or newspaper ad, but these aren't the best sources. Your chance of getting a puppy that has the best parentage, health care, and early experiences are best if you find a reputable, knowledgeable breeder. Such a breeder will be as intent upon evaluating your credentials as home for a Pekingese as you will be in evaluating them.

Show breeders: Look for responsible breeders exhibiting at dog shows, especially Pekingese specialty shows. Specialty shows are prestigious events that draw exhibitors from a wide area. You can find information about specialty shows through the Pekingese Club of America at *www.pekingeseclub.org*. This site also lists Web

"It should imply courage, boldness, and self-esteem rather than prettiness, daintiness, or delicacy." From the AKC standard.

sites and contact information for PCA members on its Breeder Referral list. If you want a show-quality Pekingese, you should subscribe to *The Orient Express* magazine, where you will find pictures of dogs and advertisements of puppies from top breeders around the country.

Questions, Questions

When you contact breeders, tell them exactly what qualities you want in a Peke, if you have a sex, color, or age preference, and whether you want pet- or show-quality. A good breeder should in turn ask you about your previous experience with dogs, why you want a Pekingese, and what living arrangements you have planned for the dog.

✔ Ask about the parents. Do they have conformation or obedience titles? This is not only important if you want a show/obedience prospect, but again can give you a clue about the care taken with the litter.

✔ What kind of temperaments do the parents and the puppies have?

✔ Have the parents or puppies had any health problems?

✔ Why did they breed the litter?

✔ How did they choose the sire?

Color choices. Pekingese come in a wide array of colors, but most people think only of the familiar black-masked fawn. True, this color does seem to highlight the Peke's oriental expression, but the angelic pure whites, enchanting soft creams, striking pitch blacks, and captivating parti-colors are all beautiful alternatives if you want something a little out of the ordinary. However, no color is considered rare, and you should avoid breeders who appear to value color over other traits.

Cost

Pekingese are relatively expensive dogs. This in part simply reflects the fact that they are expensive to produce. Cesarean sections are often needed, and litters are very small. Expect to pay at least $500 for a good pet-quality Pekingese from a good, healthy background, and $1,000 or up for a show-quality Peke. The tiny sleeve Pekes will often be even more costly. Don't expect any good breeder to sell

Don't forget the many colors Pekingese come in. But don't buy one just because the breeder claims a color is "rare."

Although similar in appearance, all puppies have different personalities.

a newcomer a true breeding-quality Peke at any (reasonable) price.

What to Look for in Peke Puppies

As you finally look upon this family of royal tumbleweeds, you may find it very difficult to be objective. How will you ever decide? If you want a show puppy, let the breeder decide. In fact, the breeder knows the puppies' personalities better than you will in the short time you can evaluate them, so listen carefully to any suggestions the breeder has, even for a pet. But first decide if this is the litter for you. Look for the following:

✔ By eight weeks of age, Peke puppies should look like little puff balls with flat faces. Dark nose pigmentation, absent at birth, should be present by this age.

✔ Normal Peke puppies are friendly, curious, and attentive. If they are apathetic or sleeping, it could be because they have just eaten, but it could also be because they are sickly.

✔ The puppies should be clean, with no missing hair, crusted or reddened skin, or signs of parasites.

✔ Eyes, ears, and nose should be free of discharge.

✔ The eyes should not bulge excessively, deviate to either side, or be reddened or crusted.

✔ Examine the eyelids to ensure that the lids or lashes don't roll in on the eye, and that the eyelids close tightly.

✔ The teeth should be straight and meet up evenly, with the bottom incisors in front of the top incisors.

✔ The gums should be pink; pale gums may indicate anemia.

✔ The area around the anus should have no hint of irritation or recent diarrhea.

✔ Puppies should not be thin or excessively potbellied. The belly should have no large bumps indicating a hernia.

✔ By the age of 12 weeks, male puppies should have both testicles descended in the scrotum.

Whichever one you choose, will be the best choice because you'll make sure your puppy will become part of your family. Of course, you could always get two...

✔ Avoid any puppy that is making significant breathing sounds, including wheezing and snorting.

✔ Avoid any puppy with pinched nostrils, especially if they appear to collapse inward as the dog inhales.

✔ If you want a profuse coat, it should already have dense, soft hair. A puppy with a sparse short coat will probably never have a lot of hair; however, think about what you really want. A thick coat can be a lot of work if all you want is a companion.

If the puppy of your choice is limping, or exhibits any of the above traits, express your concern and ask to either come back the following week to see if it has improved, or to have your veterinarian examine it. In fact, any puppy you buy should be done so with the stipulation that it is pending a health check (at your expense) by your veterinarian. The breeder should furnish you with a complete medical history including dates of vaccinations and worming.

You may still find it nearly impossible to decide which rolling dust bunny will be yours. Don't worry—no matter which one you choose, it will be the best one. In years to come you will wonder how you were so lucky to have picked the perfect Pekingese. You must realize that your Peke will be perfect in part because you are going to make it that way!

THE PEKINGESE PET

After finally locating your Peke-to-be, it's only natural to want to bring her home right away. But first channel your excitement and make sure you and your home are prepared to accept royalty.

Pekingese Purchases

It's not really true that "all you add is love" (but you'll need lots of that, too). Your new Peke puppy will need a few necessary items to get started, and you can add as many nonessentials as your budget and good sense will allow. The best places to find these items are at large pet stores, dog shows, or in discount pet catalogs.

The Lion's Den

Crate

Many new dog owners are initially appalled at the idea of putting their pet in a crate as though she were some wild beast. At times, though, even a Peke puppy can be a wild beast,

Playing in the garden is an enjoyable activity for Pekes.

and a crate is one way to save your home from ruination and yourself from insanity. A crate can also provide a quiet haven for your dog. Just as you hopefully find peace and security as you sink into your own bed at night, your puppy needs a place that she can call her own, a place she can seek out whenever she needs rest and solitude. The crate should be off-limits to children or anyone who aims to pester the dog. Used properly, your Pekingese will come to think of her crate not as a way to keep herself in, but as a way to keep others out! And by taking the puppy directly from the crate to the outdoors upon awakening, the crate will be one of the handiest house-training aids at your disposal.

Crates can be abused by overuse. The crate is not a storage box for your dog when you're finished playing with her, nor is it a place of punishment. A crate is the canine equivalent of an infant's crib—a place for naptime where you

Household Killers

- Leaked antifreeze
- Rodent baits
- Household cleaners
- Toilet fresheners
- Drugs
- Some houseplants (such as Caladium, English Holly, daffodils, Hyacinth bulbs, Philodendron, Mistletoe, and Rhododendron)
- Chocolate (especially baker's chocolate)
- Nuts, bolts, pennies
- Pins and needles
- Bones

can leave your puppy without fear of her hurting herself or your home and belongings.

Place the crate in a corner of a quiet room, but not too far from the rest of the family. Put the puppy in the crate when she begins to fall asleep, and she will become accustomed to using it as her bed. Be sure to place a soft pad in the bottom of the crate.

"X-Pen"

An exercise pen ("X-pen") is a transportable wire folding "playpen" for dogs, typically about 4 feet × 4 feet (1.22 m × 1.22 m). If you must be gone for hours at a time, X-pens are the perfect answer because the puppy can relieve herself on paper in one corner, sleep on a soft bed in the other, and frolic with its toys all over! It's like having a little yard inside your home.

Safe Places

Your new puppy should not have the run of the entire house. Choose an easily Peke-proofed room where you spend a lot of time, preferably one that is close to a door leading outside. Kitchens and dens are usually ideal. When you must leave your dog alone for some time, you may wish to place her in a crate, X-pen, or secure room. Bathrooms have the disadvantage of being so confining and isolated that puppies may become destructive; if you have no alternative, try using a secure baby gate instead of shutting the door. Garages have the disadvantage of also housing many poisonous items, as well as an array of heavy objects that could fall on an inquisitive pup.

Peke puppies should have a good supply of their own toys.

A safe haven for puppy and home: the X-pen.

Peke-proofing the Palace

Peke-proofing your home has two goals: protecting your home, and protecting your dog. Home destruction is a major reason that dogs are banished to the backyard or given up for adoption. Yet many people encourage destructive behavior by leaving such an irresistible array of alluring but forbidden objects around that the puppy never has a chance.

Get down at puppy level and see what enticements and dangers beckon. Be aware of the following:

✔ Puppies particularly like to chew items that carry your scent. Shoes, eyeglasses, and clothing must be kept out of the pup's reach.

✔ Leather furniture is the world's biggest rawhide chewy to a puppy; wicker furniture can provide hours of chewing entertainment and Pekes love to shower the room with confetti from your books and papers!

✔ Your carpets can be partially covered with small washable rugs or indoor outdoor carpeting until your puppy is house-trained. If you use an X-pen, cover the floor beneath it with thick plastic (an old shower curtain works well), and then add towels or washable rugs for traction and absorbency.

✔ Puppies love to chew electrical cords in half, and even lick outlets. These can result in severe burns, loss of the jaw and tongue, and death.

✔ Jumping up on an unstable object could cause it to come crashing down, perhaps crushing the puppy.

✔ Do not allow the puppy near the edges of high decks, balconies, or staircases.

✔ Be on the lookout for anything that might injure an eye.

Doors: Doors can be a hidden danger area. Everyone in your family must be made to understand the danger of slamming a door, which could catch a Peke puppy and seriously injure her. Use doorstops to ensure that the wind does not blow doors suddenly shut. Be especially cautious with swinging doors; a puppy may try to push one open, become caught, try to back out, and strangle. The puppy may not see clear glass doors and she could be injured running into them. Never close a garage door with your dog running around. Finally, doors leading to unfenced outdoor areas should be kept securely shut.

Peke Protection Outdoors

Your fence must not only be strong enough to keep your dog in, but to keep stray dogs out. This is why the "invisible fences" (which work

See no evil, hear no evil, say no evil. A pack of Pekes will keep you on your toes.

by shocking a dog wearing a special receiver collar when it crosses a buried boundary wire) are not recommended for Pekingese—they don't keep other animals out. If you live in a rural area, some wild animals may look upon a Peke puppy as a snack. Still, the number one predator of any dog is the automobile. Good fences don't only make good neighbors—they make live dogs!

Dangers

There can still be dangers within the yard. Bushes with sharp, broken branches at Pekingese eye level should be removed. Watch for trees with dead branches in danger of falling, or even heavy falling fruits or pinecones. If you have a pool, be aware that most Pekes are not good swimmers. A Pekingese is too small to pull itself up a swimming pool wall, and can easily drown.

Pekingese Pediatrics

Your Pekingese puppy deserves a good start in life. Your veterinarian is your best source of individualized health care, but you should be aware of the basics.

Puppy Food

Feed your young Peke puppy four times a day. From about 4 to 6 months of age, you can feed her either three or four times a day, from 6 to 9 months of age, three times a day, and then gradually cut down to twice a day by the time she's 12 months old.

Vaccinations

Without well-timed vaccinations your Pekingese can be vulnerable to deadly communicable diseases. Your puppy received her early immunity through her dam's colostrum during the first few days of nursing. As long as she still has that immunity, any vaccinations you give her won't provide sufficient immunity, but after several weeks that immunity begins to decrease. As her immunity falls, both the chance of a vaccination being effective and the chance of getting a communicable disease rise. The problem is that immunity diminishes at different times in different dogs, so starting at around six weeks of age, a series of vaccinations are given in order to catch the time when they will be effective while leaving as little unprotected time as possible. During this time of uncertainty, it's best not to take your puppy around places where unvaccinated dogs may congregate. Some deadly viruses, such as parvovirus, can remain in the soil for six months after an infected dog has shed the virus in her feces there.

Types of vaccines: This doesn't mean you must load up on every vaccine available. Vaccinations are divided into core vaccines, which are advisable for all dogs, and noncore vaccines, which are advisable only for some dogs. Core vaccines are those for rabies, distemper, parvovirus, and hepatitis (using the CAV-2 vaccine, not the CAV-1, which can cause adverse reactions and is still sold by some feed stores). Noncore vaccines include those for leptospirosis, corona virus, tracheobronchitis, Lyme disease, and giardia. Your veterinarian can advise you if your dog's lifestyle and environment put her at risk for these diseases.

A sample core vaccination protocol for puppies suggests giving a three-injection series at least two weeks apart, with each injection containing distemper (or measles for the first injection), parvovirus, adenovirus 2 (CAV-2), and parainfluenza (CPIV). The series should not end before 12 weeks of age. A booster is given one

The Homecoming Kit

- Buckle collar (cat collar for puppies)—for wearing around the house
- Lightweight leash (nylon, web, or leather, never chain!). An adjustable show lead is great for puppies.
- Stainless steel, flat-bottomed food and water bowls. Avoid plastic, which can cause allergic reactions and hold germs.
- Crate—large enough for an adult to stand up in
- Exercise pen—24 inches to 30 inches (61–76 cm) tall
- Toys—latex squeakies, fleece-type toys, ball, stuffed animals without loose eyes or other easily detached parts, stuffed socks
- Chewbones—the equivalent of a teething ring for babies; note, eating large hunks of rawhide can cause intestinal obstruction, though
- Anti-chew preparations (e.g. "Bitter Apple")
- Baby gate(s)—better than a closed door for placing parts of your home off limits
- Soft brush
- Wide-tooth comb
- Nail clippers
- Dog shampoo (tearless)
- First aid kit
- Food. Start with the same food the puppy is currently eating (ask the breeder).
- Dog bed. Many pet beds are available, but you can also use the bottom of a plastic crate, or any cozy box. But beware—wicker will most likely be chewed to shreds.
- Camera and film—telephoto lens is a necessity!

Your Pekingese puppy depends on you to make the right decisions now to ensure a healthy life for years to come.

year later, and then boosters are given every three years. Rabies should be given at 16 weeks of age, with boosters at one- to three-year intervals according to local law.

Boosters: The topic of how frequent boosters should be given is currently under scrutiny. Some owners elect to test their dogs' blood titers to various diseases to see if a booster is needed. A high titer generally indicates protection, but a low titer doesn't mean the dog isn't protected.

Dosage: Some people contend that small dogs, such as Pekingese, should get smaller doses of vaccination, but veterinarians disagree. The immune system doesn't work based on size; after all, the same amount of virus is sufficient to infect small dogs and large dogs alike.

Note: Some proponents of natural rearing condemn vaccinations and instead use homeopathic nosodes; however, no controlled

study has ever supported the effectiveness of nosodes.

Deworming

Your puppy should have been checked and dewormed if necessary before coming home with you. Most puppies have worms at some point because some types of worms lie dormant and protected in the dam until hormonal changes caused by her pregnancy activate them and enable them to infect her puppies. Your Peke can also pick up worms from the ground in places where dogs congregate. The best prevention at home is to clean up feces immediately. Some heartworm preventives also prevent many types of worms. Get your puppy regular fecal checks for worms, but don't deworm your puppy unnecessarily. Avoid over-the-counter worm medications, which are neither as safe nor as effective as those available from your veterinarian.

Common Misconceptions about Worms

✔ Misconception: A dog that is scooting its rear along the ground has worms. Although this may be a sign of tapeworms, a dog that repeatedly scoots more likely has impacted anal sacs.

✔ Misconception: Feeding a dog sugar and sweets will give it worms. There are good reasons not to feed a dog sweets, but worms have nothing to do with them.

✔ Misconception: Dogs should be regularly wormed every month or so. Dogs should be wormed when, and only when, they have been diagnosed with worms. No worm medication is completely without risk, and it is foolish to use it carelessly.

Tapeworms: If you see small, flat, white segments in your dog's stool, she may have tapeworms. Tapeworms are acquired when your puppy eats a flea, so the best prevention is flea prevention. Tapeworms require special medication to get rid of them.

Heartworm Prevention

Heartworms are carried by mosquitoes, so if there is any chance of a single mosquito biting your Peke she needs to be on heartworm preventive medication. Ask your veterinarian when she should begin taking the medication, as it may vary according to your location. Dogs over six months of age should be checked for heartworms with a simple blood test before beginning heartworm prevention. The once-a-month

Until your puppy is properly vaccinated, take precautions that she isn't exposed to strange dogs or contaminated areas.

preventive is safe, convenient, and effective. Treatment is available for heartworms, but it's far cheaper, easier, and safer to prevent them. Left untreated, heartworms can kill your dog.

Spaying and Neutering

Most pet owners will find that life with a spayed or neutered dog is much easier than life with an intact one. An intact (unspayed) female comes into estrus twice a year, usually beginning at around eight months of age. Each heat period lasts for about three weeks, during which she will have a bloody discharge that will ruin your furnishings or necessitate her being crated for three weeks or wearing little britches (which you will forget to remove when you let her out to potty, and will then have a real mess on your hands). Her scent, which she will advertise by urinating as much as possible, will mark

All else being equal, just go with your heart.

comparatively narrow pelvis makes natural birth often impossible. A planned cesarean section is comparatively safe (although Pekingese anesthesia is always a concern), but most first-time breeders wait until the dam is in trouble, when only an emergency cesarean section can save her and the puppies. Surgery under these circumstances is expensive and risky. Pekingese litters are small, averaging only two to three puppies, so breeding them to sell is not going to make you rich.

How would you find homes for the puppies? Do you trust that the people who answer your advertisements have really good homes and will give your puppy a home as good as yours? Will you commit to being responsible for that puppy's well-being for the rest of her life? Will you take every puppy back if the new owners should tire of her or otherwise not be able to keep her? Good breeders make these commitments, and more. They screen for hereditary defects, prove their dogs in some form of competition, educate themselves, and stand by their puppies for a lifetime.

Health advantages: Intact females are at increased risk of developing breast cancer and pyometra, a potentially fatal infection of the uterus. Spaying negates the possibility of pyometra, and spaying before the first season significantly reduces the chance of breast cancer. Intact males are more likely to fight, and to develop testicular cancer and prostatitis. The major drawbacks are that each procedure requires surgery and anesthesia, that many spayed and neutered dogs gain weight, and that some spayed females develop urinary incontinence (although this is a more common concern in large breeds). Talk to your veterinarian and breeder about the pros and cons.

your home as a roadside brothel, and you may have lots of uninvited canine suitors camping at your door. If you have an intact male of your own, he will drive you insane with his relentless panting, whining, shaking, and clawing. It will be the longest three weeks of your life.

Breeding: But what about breeding? Breeding Pekingese is not a casual undertaking. Besides the expense, work, and responsibility involved in breeding any dog, breeding Pekes has added concerns. The Peke's wide head and

Breeding Pekingese entails more experience than most breeds of dogs do. They often require artificial insemination and Cesarean births.

Packing Your Peke

The small size, calm demeanor, and desire to be by their owner's side make Pekingese natural traveling companions. You may find that sharing a trip with your Pekingese, especially if you would otherwise be traveling alone, can be a rewarding experience.

Riding Safely

Ideally your Pekingese should always ride with the equivalent of a doggy seat belt: the crate. Many dogs have emerged from their crates shaken but safe, from accidents that would have otherwise proved fatal. The least safe place for your Peke to ride is in the driver's lap or hanging her head out of the window. Always be careful that your Peke doesn't jump out of the car the minute you stop.

Note: Soft "sherpa" bags arc popular for travel and for carrying your peke.

Carsickness

Nothing can spoil a road trip like a carsick dog. Carsickness is a common ailment of puppies; most outgrow it, but some need car training in order to overcome it. Initial car rides should be made extremely short, with the objective being to complete the ride before the dog gets sick. Driving to a place where the dog can get out and enjoy herself before returning home also seems to help the dog look forward to car rides and overcome carsickness. Obviously your dog shouldn't have a full stomach, but sometimes just a little food in her stomach may help. Motion sickness medication may help in stubborn cases. Consult your veterinarian.

Travel is made easier and safer with a pet carrier. Traveling in warm weather requires taking precautions against heat and loss of air conditioning.

The Pekingese Travel Kit

The suitcase for a well-prepared Peke traveler should include
- First aid kit
- Heartworm preventive
- Any other medications
- Food
- Food and water bowls
- Ice packs
- Battery-powered fan
- Dog biscuits and chewies
- Grooming supplies
- Change of bedding
- Short and long leashes
- Flashlight
- Plastic baggies or other "poop" disposal items
- Moist towelettes
- Paper towels
- Health and rabies certificate

Beside the regular tags, your dog should wear identification indicating where you could be reached while on your trip, or including the address of someone you know will be at home. Bring a recent color photo in case your Peke somehow gets lost. If you are traveling by car, a jug of water from home can be a big help, as many dogs are very sensitive to changes in water and can develop diarrhea—the last thing you need on a trip.

Traveling with your Pekingese will take some planning, but you may find that the trip is much more enjoyable because of the presence of your most loyal travel companion.

Temperature

Traveling in warm weather can be dangerous for a Pekingese. In only the brief time it takes to turn off your car while getting gas, or to run inside for a rest stop, the inside of the car can become dangerously hot. Were your car to break down on the highway, it could result in a life-threatening situation for your Peke. For these reasons you should never travel without cooling equipment; at the very least you should have a cooler with ice packs in it. You can also make or purchase a crate cooling pad, which is made of absorbent gel crystals that hold moisture and remain cool for hours. Battery-powered fans are inexpensive and helpful, but don't really produce enough breeze to make them entirely

Though not noted as hiking companions, Pekingese enjoy outings in the outdoors.

satisfactory. You can also buy a small generator that can power a large fan. These may seem like extreme measures just to take a car trip, but Pekingese cannot take chances with heat.

Warning: It should go without saying that you cannot leave your Peke in the car while you go shopping, even on a cool day. The sun absorbed through the windows can heat the car to dangerous temperatures quickly.

Tattoos and Microchips

Even license tags cannot always ensure your dog's return, because they must be on the dog to be effective. Tattooing your Social Security number or your dog's registration number on the inside of its ear or thigh provides a permanent means of identification. You can also have a microchip implanted with a simple injection. Microchips and tattoos are registered with agencies that will put you in touch with anyone who reports finding your pet. You may wish to discuss these options with your veterinarian or local breeders. Most people suggest both a microchip (registered with the AKC program) and a license tag to give your pet the best chance to be found.

ROYAL DOG FOOD

Choosing a meal fit for an emperor will be your responsibility for the life of your Peke, and your Peke's life will depend in part upon the choices you make.

Nutrition

Your Peke's nutritional needs are best met by a diet rich in meat that also contains some vegetable matter. Meat is tastier to dogs, higher in protein, and more digestible (meaning smaller stools and fewer gas problems) than plant-based ingredients. A rule of thumb is that at least three of the first six ingredients of a dog food should be animal-derived.

But a balanced diet is more than just meat; it must combine protein, fat, carbohydrates, vitamins, minerals, and water. The right mix depends on various factors. Growing dogs need more protein, active dogs need more protein and fat, fat dogs need more protein and less fat, and sick dogs need reduction or addition of various ingredients according to their illnesses. When comparing commercial food

Feeding royalty need not be a challenge. Pekingese are dogs, even if they would have you believe otherwise.

labels, you have to compare their dry matter; otherwise, the higher the moisture content, the lower the nutrients levels appear.

Protein provides the building blocks for bone, muscle, coat, and antibodies. Eggs, followed by meats, have higher quality and more digestible proteins than do plant-derived proteins.

Fat provides energy and aids in the transport of vitamins. Too little fat in the diet (less than 5 percent dry matter) results in dry coats and scaly skin. Too much fat can cause diarrhea, obesity, and a reduced appetite for more nutritious foods.

Carbohydrates must be cooked for dogs to utilize them; even then, the degree of utilization depends on the carbohydrate source. Carbohydrates from rice are best utilized, followed by potato and corn, and then wheat, oat, and beans. Excessive carbohydrates in the diet can cause diarrhea and flatulence.

Vitamins A, D, E, B_1, B_2, B_{12}, niacin, pyridoxine, pantothenic acid, folic acid, and choline

Feeding Time

Very young puppies should be fed three or four times a day, on a regular schedule. From the age of three to twelve months, puppies should be fed three times daily, and after that, twice daily. Adult dogs can be fed once a day, but it is actually preferable to feed smaller meals twice a day.

Some people let the dog decide when to eat by leaving food available at all times. If you choose to let the dog "self-feed," monitor his weight to be sure he is not overindulging. Leave only dry food in the bowl as canned food spoils rapidly and becomes both unsavory and unhealthy.

are essential ingredients in canine diets. Most dog foods have these vitamins added in their optimal percentages, so that supplementing with vitamin tablets is rarely necessary.

Minerals help build tissues and organs and are part of many body fluids and enzymes.

Deficiencies or excesses can cause anemia, poor growth, strange appetite, fractures, convulsions, vomiting, weakness, heart problems, and many other disorders. Again, most commercial dog foods have minerals added in their ideal percentages. It is not a good idea to supplement your dog's diet with minerals, especially calcium.

Fiber, such as beet pulp or rice bran, is often used in weight-loss diets to give the dog a full feeling, although its effectiveness is controversial. Too much fiber causes large stool volume and can impair the digestion of other nutrients.

Water dissolves and transports other nutrients, helps regulate body temperature, and helps lubricate joints. Dehydration can cause or complicate many health problems. Keep a bowl of clean, cool water available for your dog at all times.

The Porky Peke

Proper Pekingese weight will depend upon the bone structure of the dog, with the sleeve Pekes weighing only a few pounds. The AKC standard dictates that no proper-sized Peke should weigh more than 14 pounds (6.4 kg). It's difficult to gauge Peke weight visually, but you should be able to just feel the ribs slightly when you run your hands along the rib crate, and there should be an indication of a waistline when viewed from above, with no fat deposits around the tail base, neck, or shoulders.

Overweight: If your Pekingese is overweight, try a less fattening food or feed less of your current food. Make sure also that family members aren't sneaking him tidbits. If your Peke remains overweight, seek your veterinarian's opinion. Some endocrine disorders, such as

Chinese dog food doesn't come in take out!

Pekingese, like all dogs, are carnivores and crave a meat-based diet. However, they are also omnivores and need other ingredients as well.

hypothyroidism or Cushing's disease (see page 76) can cause the appearance of obesity and should be ruled out or treated, but most cases of obesity are simply from eating more calories than are expended. The Pekingese body structure should not be asked to support excessive weight—too much weight could actually prove crippling to these dogs, as well as predisposing them to joint injuries and herniated discs.

Diet dog foods: Several commercial high-fiber, lowfat, and medium-protein diet dog foods are available, which supply about 15 percent fewer calories per pound. It is preferable to feed one of these foods rather than simply feeding less of a high-calorie food.

Treats: Many people find that one of the many pleasures of dog ownership is sharing a special treat with their pet. Rather than giving up this bonding activity, substitute a low-calorie alternative such as rice cakes or carrots. Keep the dog out of the kitchen or dining area at food preparation or meal times. Schedule a walk immediately following your dinner to get your dog's mind off your leftovers—it will be good for both of you.

The Picky Peke

The Peke that turns his nose up at his dinner is another special challenge. First make sure your Peke is not snubbing his food with good reason. Many poor-quality dog foods are not particularly tasty. Pekes don't eat so much that you can't afford to buy your dog a high-quality food. If you do have an underweight dog, try feeding puppy food; add water, milk, or canned food, and heat slightly to increase aroma and palatability.

Active dogs need extra calories.

Try a couple of dog food brands, but if your Peke still won't eat, you may have to employ some tough love. Many picky eaters are created when their owners begin to spice up their food with especially tasty treats. The dog then refuses to eat unless the treat is offered, and finally learns that if he refuses even that proffered treat, another even tastier enticement will be forthcoming.

An exception, of course, is a sick dog, in which case feeding by hand is warranted. Cat food or meat baby food are both relished by dogs and may entice a dog without an appetite to eat.

Home-prepared and Raw Diets

Home-prepared diets have the advantage of being fresh and of using human-quality ingredients. If they are prepared according to recipes devised by certified canine nutritionists, they should have the correct proportion of nutrients.

The BARF Diet

Some people prefer to feed their dogs a BARF (Bones And Raw Food) diet, with the idea that such a diet better emulates that of a wild dog. Although dogs have better resistance to bacterial food poisoning than do humans, such diets have nonetheless occasionally been associated with food poisoning, often from salmonella, in dogs. Commercially available meats may be awash in contaminated liquids. Perhaps the worst problem with the BARF diets, however, is that most people who claim to use them never bother to find a nutritionally balanced diet, but instead rely on friends who advocate a solid diet of chicken wings or some equally unbalanced diet.

Prescription Diets

Several diseases can be helped by feeding specially formulated diets. Such diets can greatly add to a sick dog's quantity and quality of life. By understanding what ingredients must be avoided in a particular illness, you may be able to include some treats in the diet as well. Prescription diets are available through your veterinarian for all these conditions. In addition, your veterinarian can give you recipes for home-prepared diets that meet these requirements.

Food allergies: Dogs that are allergic to food ingredients are typically allergic to particular proteins. By feeding a bland diet of proteins the dog has never eaten, such as venison, duck, or rabbit, the allergic symptoms (which range from diarrhea to itchiness) should subside. If they do, add ingredients back one by one until an ingredient is found that triggers the response. Some hypoallergenic diets consist not of novel proteins, but of protein molecules that are too small to cause allergic reactions.

Urinary stones: Dogs that tend to form urinary stones may be helped by diets high in certain minerals, which are usually also high in fiber. Different diets are appropriate for different types of urinary stones.

Diabetes mellitus: Diabetic dogs need diets high in complex carbohydrates, and they need to be fed on a strict schedule.

Liver disease: Dogs with liver disease must eat in order to get better, but they should avoid meat and instead get their protein from milk (unless it causes diarrhea) or soy products. They need small meals of complex carbohydrates frequently throughout the day. Vitamin A and copper levels must be kept low.

Pancreatitis: Pancreatitis is often precipitated by a high-fat meal, especially in older fatter dogs. They need to be fed a low-fat diet to lessen the likelihood of recurrence.

Congestive heart failure: Dogs with heart failure require a low-sodium diet (balanced with potassium) in order to lower their blood

CHECKLIST

Never Feed

✔ Chicken, pork, lamb, or fish bones. These can be swallowed and their sharp ends can pierce the esophagus, stomach, or intestinal walls.

✔ Any bone that could be swallowed whole. This could cause choking or intestinal blockage.

✔ Raw meat, which could contain Salmonella or other pathogens.

✔ Mineral supplements, unless advised to do so by your veterinarian.

✔ Chocolate. It contains theobromine, which is poisonous to dogs.

✔ Alcohol. Small dogs can drink fatal amounts quickly.

✔ Grapes, raisins, macadamia nuts, all of which have been implicated in dog deaths.

pressure. This will help reduce the accumulation of fluid in the lungs or abdomen.

Kidney disease: Diets for kidney disease should have moderate quantities of high-quality protein. Proteins produce toxic wastes that impaired kidneys cannot clear, causing the dog to feel ill. By feeding higher-quality protein, such as eggs—especially egg whites—beef, or chicken the fewest toxic by-products are produced in comparison to protein used. Lower levels of high-quality protein will make the dog feel better in advanced kidney failure. Controlling phosphorus, common in meats and cheeses, is an essential part of diet management. Sodium must also be kept low.

THE POLITE PEKINGESE

Like any family member, your Peke needs a set of ground rules concerning what is acceptable household behavior.

House-training

No challenge looms more ominously than house-training your new puppy. The sooner you get to it, the better it will be. In fact, puppies begin to learn to relieve themselves in specific places as early as five weeks of age, and these early places and surfaces will influence where your dog tries to relieve herself for the rest of her life. That's one reason it's so important to get your puppy from a breeder who trains her to relieve herself in a suitable place. Puppies raised in cages grow accustomed to just relieving themselves where they happen to be. Puppies raised with access to the outdoors will tend to try to go outside to relieve themselves.

Pekingese can be one of the most well-mannered canine companions, but they still need guidance.

The Proper Place

The very act of voiding in a particular place makes a puppy more likely to go there again simply because relieving herself is rewarding. Olfactory cues left from her own urine and feces also compel a puppy to use that spot again. That's why it's essential to prevent your puppy from having indoor accidents right from the start.

Unfortunately, if your puppy was raised indoors she already has plenty of rewarding experiences relieving herself inside. And there's a lot to be said for comfort and convenience, which is why we have indoor plumbing for people. And then there's the social aspect. You wouldn't expect to potty-train a child by just plopping her on a toilet and walking away; don't expect to potty-train your puppy by shoving her out the door and walking away. If you do she'll huddle by the door until she can

There are times it seems the only way to keep your floors clean is to keep your puppy in a bucket. In a sense, a crate performs that function, keeping her off your carpets when you can't pay attention.

control. A rule of thumb is that a puppy can hold itself for as many hours as the puppy is months old. That means a two-month-old can wait for two hours, or a four-month-old for four hours, up to about six months old. Always take her out before her regularly scheduled program of urinating or defecating.

The crate: You can make use of your pup's natural canine desire to keep her own den clean. If she's in her crate, she'll learn to hold herself until you let her out, as long as you don't make unreasonable demands. As she gets better at controlling herself, you can gradually enlarge her personal space. Start by placing her bed or crate in a tiny enclosed area—an area only a couple of feet beyond the boundary of her bed. Be especially vigilant so you can prevent her from soiling ther area. Once she goes several days without soiling her area, make it just a little bit larger and then larger.

Doggy door: Consider installing a doggy door that leads to a safe outdoor area. Puppies catch on to doggy doors quickly. Enclose just enough indoor area so she can get from her crate to the door.

Paper or sod square: One advantage of small dogs is that you can resort to indoor plumbing of sorts. You can opt for the old newspaper standby, but be forewarned that soiled newspapers smell horrible. Better than paper are sod squares; after all, that's what you're trying to teach her to use outside. When they're soiled, just plant them and look forward

be reunited with you, and then rush inside and go on the floor.

Instead, no matter how rushed you are or how daunting the weather, go outside with her, and when she potties outside praise her and give her a treat just as you would for any other trick you would teach her. Don't wait until she's back inside; that's too late.

Timing

Get your puppy outside as soon as she awakens, soon after she eats, in the middle of playing, or any time you see her sniffing or circling. Young puppies have poor bladder and bowel

Pekingese seem to look at home on the finest chairs. Decide now if you will allow your Peke on your furniture.

to a newly sodded yard by the time she's house-trained. Either way, start by covering the entire area and gradually reduce the size of coverage so the dog is aiming just for the paper or sod. You can also use a doggy litterbox filled with special doggy litter than is scented to attract dogs.

Accidents

No matter how hard both of you try, your puppy will almost surely have accidents. If you catch her in the act, pick her up quickly and get her outside. If you don't see her doing it, there's nothing you can do. She was not being sneaky or spiteful, and she will have no idea what your problem is if you start yelling and pointing. Such behavior will only convince her that every once in while, for no apparent rea-

son, you go insanc. Rubbing hcr nose in her mess will simply further convince her of your perverse nature.

Carpet cleaning: Puppy owners learn the secrets of carpet cleaning fast.

✔ Pick up and soak up as much of the deposit as possible. Then add a little water and again soak up as much as possible.

✔ If you have a rug cleaner that extracts liquid, now is the time to use it.

✔ Next apply an enzyme digester-type odor neutralizer (these are products specifically made for dog accidents); use enough to penetrate the pad.

✔ Leave it on for a long time, following directions. Cover the area with plastic so it doesn't dry out before the digester can break down the urine.

A Pekingese pup in "play" position.

✔ The final step is to add a nice odor, such as a mixture of lavender oil or vanilla with baking soda, to the area. Let it air out, then vacuum.

A few gifted dogs are house-trained by three months of age, but five or six months is far more common. If your Pekingese appears to urinate abnormally frequently, have your veterinarian check for a urinary tract infection.

Social Lessons

The lessons your Peke puppy learns now will shape her actions for years to come. All dogs begin life relatively fearless, gradually becoming more cautious beginning at around 12 weeks of age. By exposing your puppy to as much as possible while she's too young to be afraid, she will learn to remain unafraid of the same experiences later in life. But more than simple exposure is required—the experience must be low stress and rewarding. You should arrange to have favorable interactions with men, women, children, dogs, cats, traffic, stairs, noises, grooming, leash walking, crates, and alone time. Remember, however, that until your puppy is at least 12 weeks old and has had two sets of puppy vaccinations, you should avoid exposing her to strange dogs or places lots of dogs frequent.

Children: Children are drawn to cute puppies, so be sure your puppy isn't mobbed by a crowd of puppy petters. It's best to let your puppy meet children one by one, with both child and puppy on the ground—that way the Peke can't be stepped on or dropped. Children must be taught that puppies can't be handled roughly. Dogs and young children should always be supervised for both of their well-being. Dogs and babies should also be supervised. Always make a fuss over the dog when the baby is around so the dog will associate the baby with good times.

Being alone: Don't forget to accustom your puppy to being alone. Dogs are not naturally loners, and being alone is very stressful for them. It must be done gradually, so your puppy knows you're coming back soon. Save special interactive chew toys to occupy her when you are away. Despite your efforts, many dogs will develop separation anxiety, one of the most common causes of destructive behavior, which is also one of the most misunderstood. Some normally sedate Pekingese turn into demolition dogs when left alone. The owners attribute this Jekyll and Hyde behavior to the dog "spiting" them for leaving, or think that their dog misbehaves only then because she knows she would be caught otherwise. But an observant owner will notice some things that are different about the dog that destroys only when left alone.

Separation anxiety is characterized by lapses in house-training, nervous behavior, and destruction around doors and windows, such as chewed and scratched walls, door jambs, and rugs.

═══════════ T I P ═══════════

Training Tips
✔ Train your dog in a quiet place away from distractions. Only when your dog learns a skill very well should you gradually start practicing it in other places.

✔ Don't try to train your dog if she's tired, hot, or has just eaten. You want her peppy and hungry for your fun and treats.

✔ Don't train your dog if you're impatient or angry. You won't be able to hide your frustration, and your dog will be uneasy. Losing your cool one time can undo days of proper training.

✔ Keep your training sessions short. Dogs learn best in 10- to 15-minute sessions. Always quit while she's still having fun and doing something she can do well. You can train her several times a day if you want.

✔ You need not use a choke (or slip) collar for training. The methods you will use do not rely on snapping or tightening the collar. A buckle collar will work just as well. You will need a 6-foot (1.8-m) leash (not chain!) and maybe a 20-foot (6-m) light line.

✔ Just say a cue word once. Repeating it over and over won't help your dog learn it.

✔ Always train in gradual steps. Give rewards for getting closer and closer to the final action you want.

✔ Give the command cue just before you get the dog to do the behavior, not during or after it.

Clicker training, including "click to sit," is the most popular training method of the moment.

1. For one, the dog often appears to be in a highly agitated state when the owner returns.

2. For another, the sites of destruction are often around doors, windows, or fences, suggestive of an attempt to escape.

Such dogs are reacting to the anxiety of being left alone—remember that for a social animal this is a highly stressful situation, but the average owner, upon returning home to such ruin, punishes the dog. This in no way alleviates the anxiety of being left alone; it does, however, eventually create anxiety associated with the owner's return home, and this tends to escalate the destructive behavior.

Dogs seem to understand "when the house is in shreds and my owner appears, I get punished," but not to understand "when I chew the house it gets messed up and I will be punished when my owner appears." If they did, punishment would remedy the problem. It does not. Instead, owners must realize that they are dealing with a fear response—the fear of being alone.

Treatment: The foolhardiness of punishing a dog for being afraid should be obvious. Instead of punishing the dog, she must be conditioned to overcome her fear of separation. This is done by separating the dog for very short periods of time and gradually working up to longer periods, taking care to never allow the dog to become anxious during any session. This is complicated when the owner *must* leave the dog for long periods during the conditioning program. In these cases, the part of the house or yard in which the dog is left for long periods should be different from the part in which the

The "Stay" command is perfect for portraits.

conditioning sessions take place; the latter location should be the location in which the owner wishes to leave the dog after conditioning is completed.

In either case, when the owner returns home, no matter what the condition of the home, greet the dog calmly or even ignore her for a few minutes, to emphasize the point that being left was really no big deal. Then have the dog perform a simple trick or obedience exercise so that you have an excuse to praise her. It takes a lot of patience, and often a whole lot of self-control, but it's not fair to you or your dog to let this situation continue.

Leash Walking

Most Pekes consider themselves too proud to be led around by a leash. They will rebel and balk, unless you introduce them to leash walking so they think it's their idea.

• Many people find a harness is easier to walk a Pekingese on than a collar because it has less chance of being pulled over the head.

• If you do use a collar, choose a buckle. If you are concerned the collar may slip over the head, you can use a martingale collar, but these collars can sometimes become entangled in the hair.

• Slip collars also become entangled and can break the coat; they can also prove dangerous if you leave them on the dog unattended.

• Your leash should be nylon or leather, never chain, because chain is difficult to handle and tends to smack your dog in the face.

The first time you put a leash or collar on your Peke puppy she may roll around and bite at it. Distract her with lots of treats or even a

Being alone can be stressful.

House Soiling

If an adult dog soils the house, especially if she was previously house-trained, a veterinary exam is warranted to consider the following medical problems:

• Spayed females may dribble urine, especially when sleeping. Drug therapies can often satisfactorily treat this.

• Older dogs may not have the bladder control they once had. Consider a doggy door or litter box.

• Older dogs may have cognitive dysfunction. Drug therapy may help.

• Females, especially, may have urinary tract infections. Suspect this if she urinates small amounts frequently.

• Older dogs, especially, may have diabetes or kidney disease that cause increased thirst and urination. They need veterinary treatment.

• Intact males may be marking. Castration may help (but often does not once the habit is established).

• Intact females may be coming into estrus (heat). Spaying should help.

Also consider behavioral problems:

• Young females, especially, tend to urinate in submission upon greetings. Greet them calmly, outside if possible, and don't do anything to make them more submissive.

• Dogs of any age may be suffering from separation anxiety.

game. Have her wear it for only a short time and remove it while she's being good. Repeat several times a day until she associates a collar or harness with good times.

When you attach the leash, don't try to lead her anywhere at first. Instead, let her proudly lead you around the house and yard. If she appears glued in place, pick her up and move her to another place, or entice her to take a few steps by luring her with a treat. Gradually lure her more and more; require that she take a few steps along with you before she gets the treats—then a few more steps. Gradually she'll figure out that walking alongside you turns you into a human snack dispenser, and she'll be eager to walk alongside.

Lion Dog Training

Your Pekingese may rule your home when it comes to the small stuff, but you need to take charge when it comes to major issues. Don't expect fawning obedience, but with proper training, you can expect a partnership. No dog is perfect without guidance—not even a Pekingese. Independent and stubborn, the typical Pekingese is not the ideal candidate for Lassie's next understudy. Training using the same techniques as those used for hyperactive waggy-tailed, lick-your-boots breeds is a recipe for failure.

Pekingese Keys to Success

A big problem when training a little dog is how to guide and correct her. If you bend down to position your Pekingese every time you want her to sit, you will probably have a bad back before you have a sitting dog. Try some of these small dog solutions:

✔ Teach stationary exercises on a tabletop or other raised surface. This allows you to have eye contact with your dog and gives

Small dog training aids: a section of PVC pipe with a leash strung through it, and a light weight backscratcher or stick.

you a better vantage from which to help your dog learn.

✔ To train your dog at your feet, extend your arm length with a back scratcher with which to guide and even pet your dog without having to bend over.

✔ A leash that comes from several feet overhead has virtually no guiding ability whatsoever. You need a lower pivot point for the leash in relation to the dog, and you can achieve this by what is called a "solid leash." This is simply a hollow, light tube, such as PVC pipe, about 3 feet (0.9 m) long, through which you string your leash.

✔ To prevent a small dog from sitting or lying down, loop part of your regular leash around her belly and hold onto that part, so you have a convenient "handle."

Many breeds have difficulty mastering their impulses for perpetual motion, but not so the Peke. It is already calm, and will master the *down* or *stay* before any dog in her class, but she will also learn to be bored and start lagging before any other dog in the class. And when she plants her feet and refuses to move, you can appreciate the description of the Peke weighing far more than it would appear. Whether you want an obedience star or a well-mannered companion, every Pekingese trainer should know certain key concepts.

Think Positive!

Pekingese have gained a reputation for being difficult to train. A ranking in a popular book of most to least trainable breeds lists Pekes in the bottom 10. Anyone who has tried to force a Peke to do something it doesn't want to do is probably inclined to agree with that evaluation, but that's just it: Pekes don't respond well to force training.

Pekes respond quite well to training that makes sense to them in terms of a payoff. You don't work for free; why should your Peke? Pekingese training methods focus on fun, food, and positive associations. They produce happy, well-trained dogs that are eager to learn more. These methods use punishment only as a last resort. Punishment is good for teaching a dog to do nothing—but who wants that?

The Click Is the Trick

The most popular training method of the moment is clicker training, a type of training patterned after the way professional trainers train dolphins and other animals. It is a way of immediately signaling to your dog that her action is what you want, and that she will be rewarded for it. Ther immediate feedback helps your dog hone in on just what she's doing that brings her a reward. Otherwise, trainers have a tendency to give the reward several seconds after the desired action, often when the dog is already doing something entirely different.

By using a quick signal that your dog notices as soon as she does the right thing, you increase the accuracy of your timing. You could just say *"Good!"* and that will work, but not quite as well because your dog is so used to hearing you talk that the word doesn't stand out to her. By using a novel signal, such as a click sound, it catches your dog's attention. Here's how it works:

1. First you teach the dog that the click means *"Good!"* by clicking and immediately giving the dog a treat. You do this until the

Use a solid lead and backscratcher to extend your reach to Pekingese level.

dog looks expectantly for the treat as soon as she hears the click.

2. Now your clicker is "loaded" and you are ready to train! Be sure to click just as soon as the dog is doing what you want, and follow the click by a reward and praise.

3. You won't have to click forever. You click only to tell the dog that she has done the right thing as she is learning something.

4. After you are sure she knows how to do something, you quit giving her the click—but you still give her praise and rewards!

You can use clicker training to teach the standard commands, but you will find that

If your dog tends to sit when you want her to stand, try looping the lead around her belly until she gets the idea.

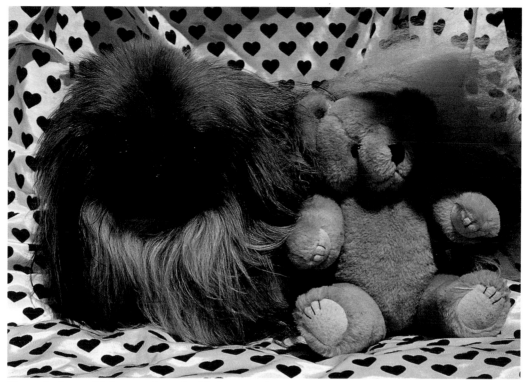

Even the best of Pekes can have bad behaviors, but in general, Pekingese are not plagued by the behavioral problems many breeds have.

your dog learns them so fast you may want to teach more. Use your imagination and teach your dog to shake, roll over, speak, play dead, or anything you can imagine. Just use the same basic shape, click, and reward concept.

Click to Sit

The old way of teaching the *sit* was to pull up on your dog's collar and push down on her rear as you said *"Sit."* It worked, but it wasn't fun. Clicking this first trick takes a little longer initially, but it lays the groundwork for super-fast learning in the long run.

One way to teach your dog to do something new is to just wait for her to do it on her own, and then quickly click and reward. This takes a lot of patience, however, so most trainers hasten it along by luring the dog into position.

✔ With her rear in a corner so she can't back up, take your treat and hold it just above and behind her nose, so she has to bend her rear legs to look up at it.

✔ Click and reward.

✔ Repeat several times, then move the treat farther back so she has to bend her legs more.

may have to prevent her from walking forward by gently restraining her with your other hand.

✔ Click and reward for just putting her nose down and forward a bit, then for reaching to the ground, then for lowering her elbows a bit, then for lying all the way down.

✔ Once she's doing that, click and reward only for doing it when you give the cue: *"Pekaboo, down!"* Then try it on different surfaces.

✔ Once again, you've taught your dog to do something useful without jerking or wrestling.

Click to Stay

Normally when you teach your dog to *sit* or *down*, she should stay in position until you give a click, which is her release signal, so once your dog knows *sit* or *down*, wait a few seconds after she's in position before clicking and rewarding. Tell her *"Stay"* (this command doesn't use her name in front of it, because some dogs tend to jump up when they hear their name) and gradually lengthen the time she must stay before getting the click and reward.

✔ Step out just in front of her to face her, then pivot back in place before clicking and rewarding.

✔ Gradually step a little farther and farther away, and return to her by circling behind. Click and reward.

✔ Go a little farther away, or stay a little longer time, but remember, it's better for her to succeed than to fail, so don't push her limits. If she does get up, simply put her back in position and have her stay a shorter time.

✔ Keep on until she has to sit.

✔ Only when she is sitting reliably to the treat lure do you introduce a cue word: *"Pekaboo, sit."* Gradually fade out use of the treat lure, using just your hand at first, then nothing. Be sure to continue giving it as her final reward, though.

✔ Congratulations! You've taught your Peke to sit without jerking on her collar or pushing on her rear. She probably thinks this is pretty fun. On to the next trick!

Click to Down

✔ With your dog sitting or standing, use your treat to lure her nose down and forward. You

Click to Heel

Your aim in *heeling* is to have your dog walk abreast of your left leg.

✔ If your dog isn't leash-trained, place her on a leash and just walk with her. Click and reward when she's by your side.

✔ Show her a treat and encourage her to walk a few feet with you for it. Click and reward.

✔ Work up to slightly longer distances. If she balks or fights the lead, just stop or go in a different direction.

✔ You can perfect her position by rewarding only when she is by your left leg.

✔ Again, shape her gradually to get to that point. Once there, introduce the cue, *"Pekaboo, heel!"*

✔ If she insists on pulling you to investigate sights and smells, turn away from what she wants and ask her to *heel*.

✔ Once she does so, click and reward her by saying *"OK"* and letting her go investigate.

✔ Gradually require her to walk a few steps toward the object without pulling before giving her the click and OK.

Teach tricks by guiding your Peke with a small treat. To teach "sit up," hold the treat over your Peke's head and give it to her as soon as she sits up. Then gradually require her to sit up longer before rewarding her. But don't ask her to sit up for too long; the Peke is not really built for this position.

Click to Come

Coming when called is not a compromise— your dog already knows how to come when she sees you setting down her dinner. Your job is to make her want to come that eagerly every time you call her. You do this by making it rewarding to come to you.

✔ Keep some treats in your pocket, and don't be stingy with them when she comes to you. Even if she's been up to mischief, be sure not to reprimand her when she comes. Your dog is smart enough to figure out she would be better off staying away next time.

✔ If you have a helper, you can play a game that will get your Peke really running to you. In an enclosed area, such as a hallway, have your friend hold your dog while you show her a treat or toy.

✔ Back away, enticing her until she's struggling to get to you. Then call out, *"Pekaboo, come!"* and turn and run away from her just as your friend releases her. As she gets to you, click and give her the treat. Make a game out of running faster and farther away from her. Always quit while she still wants to play more.

How do you see eye to eye with a member of another species when you live in two very different worlds? You will be teaching your dog your human language; take the time to learn to speak Peke.

Translating "Peke Speak"

Like their wolf ancestors, Pekes depend upon facial expressions and body language in social interactions:

✔ A yawn is often a sign of nervousness. Drooling and panting can indicate extreme nervousness or motion sickness.

✔ A wagging tail, lowered head, and exposed teeth upon greeting are signs of submission.

✔ The combination of a lowered body, wagging tucked tail, urination, and perhaps even rolling over are signs of extreme submission.

✔ The combination of exposed teeth, a high, rigidly held tail, raised hackles, very upright posture, stiff-legged gait, direct stare, forward raised ears, and perhaps lifting his leg to urinate indicates very dominant, threatening behavior.

✔ The combination of a wagging tail, front legs and elbows on the ground and rear in the air, with or without vocalizations is the classic "play-bow" position, and is an invitation for a game.

The Pekingese conformation makes some of its body language a little more subtle than that of most other breeds. But Peke owners soon become adept at reading their friends.

A Peke's Eye View

Your Pekingese not only speaks a different language

The nervous dog will pant, drool, and shake, as well as hold its ears back and down.

than you do, but she lives in a different sensory world.

Olfaction

Short-nosed breeds, such as the Pekingese, have less olfactory area and fewer olfactory receptors than do longer-nosed breeds, and some researchers have proposed that they may not have quite as acute a sense of smell as longer-nosed breeds. This has not been proven, however, and, regardless, the Pekingese scenting ability is so vastly superior to ours that any small differences between breeds is hardly worth pointing out. After all, most people don't get a Pekingese with the idea of using it as a hunting dog.

Taste

Dogs also have a well developed sense of taste, and have most of the same taste receptors that we do. Research has shown that they

Extreme submissive pose.

prefer meat (not exactly earth-shaking news), and while there are many individual differences, the average dog prefers beef, pork, lamb, chicken, and horsemeat, in that order.

Dogs have sugar receptors similar to ours, which explains why many have a sweet tooth. But their perception of artificial sweeteners is not like ours, and seem to taste bitter to them.

Vision

Dogs do not see the world with as much detail or color as humans do. The dog's sense of color is like that of a "color-blind" person. That is, they confuse similar shades of yellow-green, yellow, orange, and red, but can readily see and discriminate blue, indigo, and violet from all other colors and each other.

The dog's vision is superior when it comes to seeing in very dim light. The eyeshine you may see from your dog's eyes at night is from a structure that serves to increase her ability to see in the dark.

Hearing

Dogs can hear much higher tones than humans can, and so can be irritated by high hums from your TV or from those ultrasonic flea collars. The Peke's drop ears may somewhat encumber its sense of hearing, but the effect is very small.

Pain

Many dogs are amazingly stoic. Because a dog may not be able to express that it is in pain, you must be alert to changes in your dog's demeanor. A stiff gait, low head carriage, reluctance to get up, irritability, dilated pupils, whining, or limping are all indications that your dog is in pain.

The classic "play-bow" position.

Lost in Translation

Your Peke is adept at noticing your body language, but is she reading what you want her to?

✔ In human culture, looking somebody directly in the eye is a sign of sincerity; in dog culture, it's a threat.

✔ In human culture, striding right up to somebody to make introductions is considered polite; in dog culture, it's rude.

✔ In human culture, bending forward is only natural when we try to call a child to us; in dog culture, it pushes them away.

✔ In human culture, slapping someone on the back or tousling them on top of the head is a sign of affection; in dog culture, it's a statement of dominance.

✔ In human culture, hugging people is a way to make them feel more secure; in dog culture, it makes them uncomfortable.

IN THE PEAK OF CONDITION

The Peke's crowning glory, that majestic mane and coat, needs a short grooming session about twice a week if it is to remain in all its glory.

The Lion's Mane

Many dogs and owners look forward to grooming sessions as a relaxing time of bonding. The upkeep of a Pekingese requires a little grooming often, rather than a lot of grooming seldom.

Grooming even the lushest of coats requires only a wide-tooth comb, natural bristle brush, and a water spritzer bottle. You may wish to use a grooming table or other raised surface, but it is equally effective to have the dog lie on your lap while being brushed.

If you start by grooming your puppy before he's had time to develop any tangles, your puppy will come to think of being brushed as something that feels wonderful. Keep each session short, fun, and rewarding. With the young puppy, you need not follow the full grooming routine; remember, although you certainly

Beautiful coats come from good genes and good care.

want to prevent the formation of any tangles, your most important long-term goal now is training the puppy to be cooperative.

Hold the puppy on your lap and accustom him to being petted or brushed, not only while he's right side up, but also while lying on his back. The fluffy puppy coat is actually more prone to matting than the adult coat is, especially at the transitional period from puppy to adult coat.

Hair and hygiene: Peke puppies sprout hair rapidly, and some of it grows in inopportune areas. The hair around the anus and the end of the sheath of the penis can accumulate waste matter. If this is a problem, you can carefully scissor the hair from these delicate regions. Even so, you will need to check these areas every time your Peke returns from relieving himself.

The feet: A typical and desirable trait of the Peke coat is the long hair of the feet. Sometimes the hair on the bottom of the feet can cause a dog to slip on a slick floor, and you

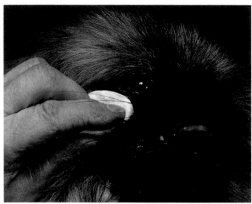

The facial fold must be wiped clean daily. Combine it with a treat so your Peke reminds you.

may want to carefully scissor that hair so that the pads can provide traction.

The face: Your puppy must also allow you to clean his face regularly. The skin in the wrinkle over the nose should be cleaned and dried once or twice daily using a cotton ball. If left unattended, moisture will accumulate and ultimately lead to a very unpleasant odor and possibly infection. Any discharge from the eyes should be wiped away with a moist cotton ball. Cleaning your Peke's face should become a routine for the entirety of your Peke's life.

Brushing

The Pekingese is blessed with a thick double coat, consisting of a soft, fine undercoat for warmth and a longer, coarse weather-resistant overcoat. Some people make the mistake of brushing only the outer coat, inadvertently allowing the undercoat to mat. For this reason you must brush the coat in layers, taking care that the hair is brushed all the way down to the skin.

✔ Begin brushing at the face, moving to the rear on one side of the dog, and then the other.
✔ Finally, turn the dog over and brush the underside.
✔ Before brushing, mist the coat with a light spray of water or coat conditioner. This helps prevent static electricity and lessens coat breakage.
✔ After brushing, repeat the process using the wide-tooth comb, to make sure that no tangles remain.
✔ As your finishing touch, mist the coat again and brush the hair on the top of the body from the skull back to the end of the tail in the direction of hair growth.
✔ Brush all of the hair in the rear half of the dog (all areas behind the rib crate) in the direction of growth. The exception is the coat on the backs of the thighs, which should be brushed upward.
✔ The coat on the sides of the body over the rib cage and on the forechest should also be brushed up and forward, emphasizing the width of the chest.
✔ Finally, place the tail over the back and brush the hair in the direction of growth, which will now be toward the head.

Note: Some cornstarch sprinkled into the coat and brushed out can help the hair to fluff, and is especially useful for the areas behind the ears, on the tail, and hind leg hair, but repeated use can dry the hair.

Coat Disasters

• Wet or muddy hair can be dried and cleaned by sprinkling a liberal amount of cornstarch, rubbing it in, and brushing it out.
• Pine tar can be loosened with hair spray.

The Pekingese has thick undercoat, with a long, coarse, straight outer coat that stands off from the body, forming a mane around the shoulders.

• Other tar can be worked out with vegetable oil, followed by dishwashing detergent.

• Tight mats and burrs can be helped by soaking them for an hour in tangle remover or vegetable oil.

• Chewing gum can be eased out by first applying ice.

Mats: You may discover some matting behind the ears or under the elbows. The coat is more prone to mat during shedding season or when it is oily or dirty. Never wash a matted coat, which only causes the mat to become more tightly bound. Try to split a mat with your fingers, starting near either end and pulling it in half longitudinally. Hold the hair between the mat and your dog's skin to avoid painful pulling. More stubborn mats may require splitting with a rake (a wooden brush with hard metal teeth), or, as a last resort, scissors. Even with scissors, split the mat into halves; don't just cut it out. To avoid accidentally cutting the skin, wriggle a fine comb between the mat and the skin before you start snipping.

Shedding: This is controlled not by exposure to warmer temperatures, but by exposure to longer periods of light. This is why indoor dogs, which are exposed to artificial light, tend to shed somewhat all year. Pekes have a heavier shedding session once a year, or following every estrus in females, during which time the flying hairs and matting can be overwhelming. Brush every day.

When matting is extensive or fleas are overwhelming, shaving the coat may be the only

alternative. It is sometimes argued that a dog's coat acts as insulation and helps keep the dog cool in summer, but as long as the coat is not shaved to the skin, little insulation will be lost.

Bathing

The two cardinal rules of bathing are: **1.** never bathe a matted coat; and **2.** never bathe a shedding coat unless you have first brushed out every loose hair.

Dirty and oily hair has an unpleasant smell and is more likely to mat. Frequent grooming will lessen the need for frequent bathing. For the average well-kept Peke, there should be no need to bathe more than once every couple of months.

Shampoo: You will get better results with a shampoo made for dogs. Dog skin has a pH of 7.5, while human skin has a pH of 5.5; thus, bathing in a shampoo formulated for the pH of human skin can lead to scaling and irritation.

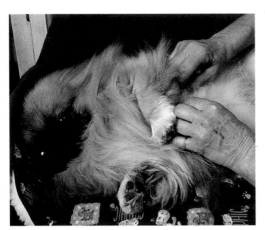

Check in the armpit area for mats. Check everywhere else, too.

Most shampoos will kill fleas even if not especially formulated as a flea shampoo, but none has any residual killing action on fleas. Therapeutic shampoos are available to aid skin problems. Dry, scaly skin is treated with moisturizing shampoos, excessive scale and dandruff with antiseborrheic shampoos, damaged skin with antimicrobials, and itchy skin with oatmeal-based antipruritics. Finally, all Peke owners should have on hand one of the shampoos

that requires no water or rinsing. These are wonderful for puppies, spot baths, emergencies, and bathing when time does not permit.

Training: Even the most devoted of owners seldom look forward to bathtime. Unfortunately, most owners train their dogs to hate baths through improper early bath training. They put off giving a bath, and when they do, they figure that by making it a thorough bath, the results will somehow last longer. The secret is to give lots of tiny baths, so tiny the puppy doesn't have a chance to get scared. Rinse (don't even wash) one leg today, an ear tomorrow, and so on. Be firm, soothing, and playful. A sink with a hand-held spray is most convenient.

Once you have worked up to a full-scale bath, begin with a thorough brushing to remove tangles and distribute oils, then wet your dog down, working forward from the rear. Use water that would be comfortable for you to bathe in, and be sure to keep some running on your hand in order to monitor any temperature changes. A fractious Peke could inadvertently hit a faucet knob and cause himself to be scalded. If you keep one hand on your dog's neck or ear, he is less likely to splatter you with a wet dog shake.

Once soaked, use your hand or a soft brush to work in the shampoo (it will go a lot farther and be easier to apply if you first mix the shampoo with warm water). Pay special attention to the oily area around the ear base, but avoid getting water in the dog's ears (try plugging them with cotton). Rinse thoroughly, this time working from the head back. A cream rinse is optional.

The finished coat is combed in such a way as to emphasize its fullness.

Itchy skin is often caused by allergies, including allergies to pollen, house dust, or flea bites. Scratching breaks the coat off.

Drying: When towel drying, be sure not to rub to the point of creating tangles. The coat will look even better if you blow it dry while brushing the hair backward. Again, you must accustom your dog to a blow dryer gradually, and always keep your hand at the place on the dog you are drying; once your hand gets uncomfortably hot, you know the dog's skin must also be uncomfortable. A high-velocity dryer, which dries by blowing air at high speed rather than by blowing hot air, is better. Blow in a steady direction to avoid tangling.

Skin and Coat Problems

FAD: Skin problems in all dogs are the most common problems seen by veterinarians, and the most common of all skin problems is *flea allergy dermatitis* (FAD). Itchy, crusted bumps with hair loss in the region around the rump, especially at the base of the tail, result from a flea bite anywhere on the dog's body.

Allergic reactions: Besides FAD, dogs can have allergic reactions to pollens or other inhaled allergens. Food allergies can also occur, but are uncommon.

Pyoderma, with pus-filled bumps and crusting, is another common skin disease. *Impetigo* is characterized by such bumps and crusting most often in the groin area of puppies. Both are treated with antibiotics and antibacterial shampoos.

Hot spots: A reddened moist itchy spot that suddenly appears is most likely a "hot spot," which arises from an itch-scratch-chew cycle resulting most commonly from fleas or flea allergy. Clip the surrounding hair, wash the area with an oatmeal-based shampoo, and prevent the dog from further chewing. A distasteful product such as Bitter Apple may dissuade the dog from chewing. Many breeders use Listerine mouthwash or Gold Bond powder with good results. Your veterinarian can also prescribe antiinflammatory medication.

Seborrhea: In seborrhea, there may be excessive dandruff or greasiness, often with a great deal of ear wax and a rancid odor. Treatment is with antiseborrheic shampoos.

Disease: Hair may be lost due to hypothyroidism, Cushing's syndrome, ovarian cysts, or testicular tumors.

Skin Problems

A healthy coat depends on healthy skin. Skin allergies, parasites, and infections can make your dog's skin unhealthy and your dog uncomfortable.

Allergies

Suspect an allergy if your Pekingese has reddened itchy skin, particularly around the ears, eyes, feet, forelegs, armpits, and abdomen. The dog may scratch and lick, and rub his torso or rump on furniture or rugs.

Allergens: Pollens and other inhaled microscopic items, chemicals on rugs and lawns, various foods, and fleas are all common allergens. The most common inhaled allergens are dander, pollen, dust, and mold. They are often seasonal. Unlike in humans, where hay fever and other inhaled allergens typically cause sneezing, in dogs they more often cause itching. Allergens can be isolated with a skin test in which small amounts of allergen extracts are injected under the skin, which is then monitored for reactions. Besides avoiding allergens, some treatments are available. Treatment includes antihistamines, glucocorticoids, and hyposensitization.

Flea allergy dermatitis (FAD), which is an allergic reaction to the saliva that a flea injects under the skin whenever it feeds, is the most common allergy among dogs. Not only does it cause intense itching in that area, but all over the dog, especially around the rump, legs, and paws. Even a single flea bite can cause severe reactions in allergic dogs.

Fleas

New products have made the age-old curse of fleas finally manageable. These products have a higher initial purchase price compared to traditional products but are cheaper in the long run because they work and they need be reapplied only every few months. Most of these products are available only from your veterinarian, although some discount products try to sound like they work the same. Look for a product with one of the following ingredients:
• Imidacloprid: a self-distributing liquid that kills fleas within a day and continues for a month. It can withstand water, but not repeated bathing.
• Fipronil: a spray or self-distributing liquid that collects in the hair follicles and wicks out over time. It kills fleas for up to three months and ticks for a shorter time, and is resistant to bathing.
• Selamectin: a self-distributing liquid that kills fleas for one month. It also kills ear mites and several internal parasites, and acts as a heartworm preventive.
• Nytenpyram: oral medication that starts killing fleas in 20 minutes; all fleas are killed in four

hours. It has almost no residual activity, so it's mostly for a quick fix of heavily infested dogs.

• Lufenuron, methoprene, or fenoxycarb: chemicals that interfere with the hatching of flea eggs.

Most over-the-counter products are permethrin-based, which isn't resistant to water and doesn't kill fleas for long. Flea populations can easily become resistant to it. In fact, fleas can become resistant to any treatment, so the best strategy is to change products frequently and to include the use of both a flea killer and a flea egg killer.

Ticks

Ticks are harder to kill than fleas. The same fipronil flea product will kill ticks, but not immediately. Amitraz tick collars are also effective, but not perfect. Regardless, if you're in a tick-infested area you'll need to supplement by feeling your Peke daily (he'll like the extra petting), paying close attention around the ears, neck, and between the toes.

Diseases: Ticks can transmit several diseases. A vaccination is available for Lyme disease, but it's not advisable for dogs that don't live in Lyme endemic areas. Of greater concern is erhlichiosis, a potentially fatal disease that cripples the immune system and often has vague symptoms. Other tick-borne diseases include Rocky Mountain Spotted Fever and babesiosis. Your veterinarian can order blood tests if these conditions are suspected.

Mites

Mites can also cause problems. Sarcoptic mites cause sarcoptic mange, an intensely itchy disorder that you can catch. It's often characterized by

Try to be vigilant about checking your Peke's coat for skin problems.

small bumps and crusts on the ear tips, abdomen, elbows, and hocks. The condition can be treated with repeated shampoos or with drugs.

Demodex mites cause demodectic mange, a noncontagious but often difficult-to-treat condition. A couple of small patches in a puppy are commonplace and will usually go away on their own, but many such patches or a generalized condition must be treated with repeated dips or with drug therapy. Cases involving the feet can be especially difficult to cure.

The Hidden Bear Claws

The long hair of the feet may hide the toenails, causing many owners to neglect cutting the nails as often as needed. When you can hear the pitter-patter of clicking nails, that means that with every step the nails are hitting the floor, and when this happens, the bones of the foot are spread, causing discomfort and eventually splayed feet and lameness. If dewclaws are left untrimmed, they can get caught on things more easily or actually loop around and grow into the dog's leg. You must prevent this by trimming your dog's nails every week or two.

✔ Begin by handling the feet and nails daily, and then cutting the very tips of your puppy's nails every week, taking special care not to cut the "quick" (the central core of blood vessels and nerve endings).

✔ You may find it easiest to cut the nails with your Pekingese lying on his back in your lap.

✔ If you look at the bottoms of the nails, you will see a solid core culminating in a hollowed nail. Cut the tip up to the core, but not beyond.

✔ On occasion, you will slip up and cause the nail to bleed. This is best stopped by styptic powder, but if this is not available, dip the nail in flour or hold it to a wet teabag.

Dental Care

Pekes have a tendency to lose teeth at an early age, but you can do your best to delay such losses by good dental care.

Baby teeth: Between four and seven months of age, Peke puppies will begin to shed their baby teeth and show off new permanent teeth. Often, deciduous (baby) teeth, especially the canines (fangs), are not shed, so that the permanent tooth grows in beside the baby tooth. If this condition persists for over a week, consult your veterinarian. Retained baby teeth can cause misalignment of adult teeth, and are of special concern in toy and brachycephalic breeds, such as the Pekingese.

Occlusion: Correct occlusion is important for good dental health. In a correct Peke bite, the top incisors should be behind the bottom incisors. This prognathic (undershot) bite is common to brachycephalic breeds. Too large a gap between the upper and lower incisors could cause eating difficulties or result in the tongue lolling out of the mouth.

Check for rotated teeth, seen most often in the upper jaw of brachycephalic breeds. Such teeth are more prone to increased plaque formation, and may need to be removed for the sake of oral hygiene.

Hygiene: Pekingese can have a problem with plaque and tartar accumulation, which worsens

Cut the nails as close to the "quick" as possible.

Open wide! Dental care is essential for good health.

with increasing age. Dry food, hard dog biscuits, and rawhide chewies are helpful, but not totally effective, at removing plaque. Brushing your Peke's teeth once or twice weekly (optimally, daily) with a child's toothbrush and doggy toothpaste is the best plaque remover. If not removed, plaque will attract bacteria and minerals, that will harden into tartar.

If you cannot brush, your veterinarian can supply a cleansing solution that will help to kill plaque-forming bacteria, as well as bad breath! You may have to have your veterinarian clean your dog's teeth as often as once a year.

Neglected plaque and tartar can cause infections to form along the gum line. The infection can gradually work its way down the sides of the tooth until the entire root is undermined. The tissues and bone around the tooth erode, and the tooth finally falls out. Meanwhile, the bacteria may have entered the bloodstream and been carried throughout the body, causing infection in the kidneys and heart valves. Neglecting your dog's teeth can do more harm than causing bad breath—it could possibly kill your dog.

Ear Care

The dog's ear canal is made up of an initial long vertical segment that then abruptly angles to run horizontally toward the skull. This configuration, along with hanging hairy ear flaps, provides a moist environment in which various ear infections can flourish.

Ear problems: Signs of ear problems include inflammation, discharge, foul odor, pain, scratching, shaking, tilting of the head, or circling to

one side. Extreme pain may indicate a ruptured eardrum. Ear problems can be difficult to cure once they have become established, so early veterinary attention is crucial. Bacterial and fungal infections, ear mites or ticks, foreign bodies, inhalant allergies, seborrhea, or hypothyroidism are possible underlying problems.

Note: Use cotton swabs with caution in the ear canal, as they can irritate the skin and pack debris into the horizontal canal. Never use powders in the ear, which can cake, or hydrogen peroxide, which leaves the ear moist. A Peke with ear problems can benefit from having his ears bound over his head for a few hours each day to aerate and dry the canals.

Ear mites: Highly contagious and intensely irritating, ear mites are often found in puppies. Affected dogs will shake their head, scratch their ears, and carry their head sideways. A dark, dry, waxy buildup in the ear canal, usually of both ears, is the ear mite's signature. If you

place some of this wax on a piece of dark paper, and have very sharp eyes, you may be able to see the tiny white culprits moving.

Over-the-counter ear mite preparations can cause worse irritation, so ear mites should be treated by your veterinarian. Separate a dog with ear mites from other pets and wash your hands after handling its ears.

Eye Care

The Pekingese eye is subject to more problems than that of most breeds. Special care must be taken to prevent corneal abrasions. Even the Peke's own hair can be an irritant, and long hair should never be allowed to hang over his eyes. The hair of the over-nose wrinkle can grow into the eye unless it is trained daily by pressing the hair of the wrinkle together, or by very carefully snipping it shorter with blunt-nosed scissors.

The Peke's prominent eyes are targets for corneal abrasions.

Corneal Abrasions

These are more common in dogs with bulging eyes, and Pekes from today's better breeders have less bulgy eyes than typical poorly bred Pekes do. But in any Peke, corneal abrasions can occur.

Blinking, tearing, or an aversion to bright light are all signs of discomfort. Examine the cornea (the clear outer surface of the eye) for minute indentations, scratches, or discolored areas that are the early signs of corneal ulcerations. If an ulceration is neglected, the entire cornea can turn whitish in a very short time, and permanent scarring of the cornea can occur even after the eye heals.

Pigment granules can appear in the scarred areas and proliferate. In a condition called *pannus*, the cornea becomes progressively covered with pigment or blood vessels, sometimes to the point that the dog becomes completely blind.

Treatment: This should be under a veterinarian's supervision. As a first step, you can flood the eye with sterile saline solution (such as that available for contact lens wearers) and apply an ophthalmic ointment. Keep the dog out of bright light and prevent him from pawing his eye. An Elizabethan collar is available from your veterinarian that will prevent your dog from reaching his head with his feet. If your dog has dewclaws, you can wrap self-clinging tape (such as Vet-Wrap) around the dog's wrist.

Eyelid anomolies: Sustained tearing of the eye could be due to eyelid anomalies that irritate the cornea; if ignored, they could injure the eye to the point of causing blindness. Examine your

Peke's eye with a magnifying glass to see if any lashes or hairs from the over-nose wrinkle are turned inward toward the eye (trichiasis), or if there is an abnormal row of lashes (distichiasis—most often on the outer half of the upper lid), or if there is a hair growing from the caruncle, or if the lid itself turns in into the eye (entropion—most often in the middle of the lower lid). These are all serious conditions that may require surgery to prevent extreme discomfort and possible blindness.

A watery discharge: This can be a symptom of a foreign body, allergies, or a tear drainage problem. If accompanied by squinting or pawing, suspect a foreign body in the eye. Examine under the lids and flood the eye with saline solution, or use a moist cotton swab to remove any debris. A clogged tear drainage duct can cause the tears to drain into the face, rather than the normal drainage through the nose. In some Pekingese, the duct may be abnormally small or not present at all. Your veterinarian can diagnose a drainage problem with a simple test.

KCS: A thick ropey mucus or crusty discharge suggests conjunctivitis or dry eye (keratoconjunctivitis sicca, or KCS). In KCS there is inadequate tear production, resulting in irritation to the surface of the eye whenever the dog blinks. The surface of the eye may appear dull. KCS can cause secondary bacterial infection or corneal ulcers. In fact, KCS should be suspected in any dog in which recurrent corneal ulceration or conjunctivitis is a problem.

In past years, treatment of KCS was with the frequent application of artificial tears, which most owners found difficult to perform as often as needed. Recent drug advances treat the causes of KCS with ophthalmic immunosuppressive therapy. This therapy can be quite effective

if begun early enough, but if you wait until the deeper layers of the cornea are affected, there may be irreversible damage. Therefore, it is imperative that you seek veterinary attention when your Peke has symptoms of KCS.

Lens problems: As your Peke ages, it is natural that the lens of the eye becomes a little hazy. You will notice this as a slightly grayish appearance behind the pupils. But if this occurs at a young age, or if the lens looks white or opaque, ask your veterinarian to check your Peke for cataracts. In cataracts, the lens becomes so opaque that light can no longer reach the retina; as in humans, the lens can be surgically replaced with an artificial lens.

Prolapse: Because of the Peke's relatively large eyes and shallow eye sockets, it is entirely possible for prolapse of the eye to occur, in which the eyeball actually pops out of the socket in response to a blow to the head. This is obviously an emergency that requires immediate veterinary attention if there is to be any hope of saving the dog's vision. Sometimes the eye will slide back if you pull the lids wide apart, but the more you handle the lids and eye, the more the area will swell, and the more you risk injuring the eye. If it doesn't work with the first try, cover the globe with a moist sponge and get to the veterinarian. The dog may have to be sedated to replace the eye.

Sometimes the eye is so injured that sight is never regained; occasionally, the eye itself must be removed. The faster treatment is obtained, the better the chance of recovery.

Pupils: Any time your dog's pupils do not react to light, or when one eye reacts differently from another, take it to the veterinarian immediately. It could indicate a serious ocular or neurological problem.

IN SICKNESS AND IN HEALTH

Your Peke is almost human, and like humans, she can get sick. Unlike humans, she can tell you where he hurts only if you know how to listen. By knowing the signs of illness, when to call the veterinarian, and how to be a doggy nurse, you can help your Pekingese stay healthy.

Pekingese Veterinarians

Don't wait until your dog is sick to choose a veterinarian. Consider availability, emergency arrangements, facilities, costs, ability to communicate, and experience with Pekingese or other brachycephalic breeds. Most general veterinarians can provide a wide range of services, but if your dog has a problem that eludes diagnosis or requires specialized treatment, let your veterinarian know if you are willing to be referred to a specialist in that field.

Signs of Sickness

Since your Peke can't talk, you have to interpret her behavioral and physical signs. Sick

Good health is the result of good genes, good care, and good luck.

dogs often lie quietly in a curled position. Dogs in pain may be irritable, restless, and may hide, pant, claw, and tremble. Dogs with abdominal pain often stretch and bow. A dog with breathing difficulties will often refuse to lie down, or if she does, will keep her head raised. Confusion, head pressing, or seizures may indicate neurological problems.

Lethargy is the most common sign of illness. Possible causes include
- Infection (check for fever)
- Anemia (check gum color)
- Circulatory problem (check pulse and gum color)
- Pain (check limbs, neck, back, mouth, eyes, ears, and abdomen for signs)
- Nausea
- Poisoning (check gum color and pupil reaction; look for vomiting or abdominal pain)

The Five Minute Checkup

Make several copies of this checklist and keep a record of your dog's home exams.

Date: _____

Weight: _____

Temperature: _____

Pulse: _____

Behavior

Is your dog
- ☐ Restless? ☐ Lethargic?
- ☐ Weak? ☐ Dizzy?
- ☐ Irritable? ☐ Confused?
- ☐ Bumping into things?
- ☐ Trembling? ☐ Pacing?
- ☐ Hiding? ____
- ☐ Eating more or less than usual?
- ☐ Drinking more than usual?
- ☐ Urinating more or less than usual, or with straining?
- ☐ Having diarrhea?
- ☐ Straining to defecate?
- ☐ Just standing with front feet on ground and rear in the air?
- ☐ Vomiting or trying to vomit?
- ☐ Regurgitating undigested food?
- ☐ Gagging? ☐ Coughing?
- ☐ Breathing rapidly at rest?
- ☐ Spitting up froth?
- ☐ Pawing at throat?
- ☐ Snorting?
- ☐ Limping?

Physical Exam

Hydration: ☐ Dry sticky gums?
 ☐ Skin that doesn't pop back when stretched?

Gum color: ☐ Pink (good) ☐ Bright red ☐ Bluish ☐ Whitish ☐ Red spots

Gums: ☐ Swellings? ☐ Bleeding? ☐ Sores? ☐ Growths?

Teeth: ☐ Loose? ☐ Painful? ☐ Dirty? ☐ Bad breath?

Nose: ☐ Thick or colored discharge? ☐ Cracking? ☐ Pinched? ☐ Sores?

Eyes: ☐ Tearing? ☐ Mucous discharge? ☐ Dull surface? ☐ Squinting? ☐ Swelling? ☐ Redness? ☐ Unequal pupils? ☐ Pawing at eyes?

Ears: ☐ Bad smell? ☐ Redness? ☐ Abundant debris? ☐ Scabby ear tips? ☐ Head shaking? ☐ Head tilt? ☐ Ear scratching? ☐ Painfulness?

Feet: ☐ Long or split nails? ☐ Cut pads? ☐ Swollen or misaligned toes?

Skin: ☐ Parasites? ☐ Black grains (flea dirt)? ☐ Hair loss? ☐ Scabs? ☐ Greasy patches? ☐ Bad odor? ☐ Lumps?

Anal and genital regions:
 ☐ Swelling? ☐ Discharge?
 ☐ Redness? ☐ Bloody urine?
 ☐ Bloody or blackened diarrhea?
 ☐ Worms in stool or around anus?
 ☐ Scooting rear?
 ☐ Licking rear?

Abdomen: ☐ Bloating?

Body: ☐ Asymmetrical bones or muscles? ☐ Lumps? ☐ Weight change?

- Sudden vision loss
- Cancer
- Metabolic diseases

If you answered "yes" to anything abnormal in the checklist, it's worth a call to your veterinarian.

Temperature

To take your dog's temperature, lubricate a rectal thermometer and insert it about 2 inches (5 cm) into the dog's anus, leaving it there for about a minute. Normal is from 101 to 102°F (38.3–38.9°C). If the temperature is

✔ 103°F (39.4°C) or 104°F, call your veterinarian for advice.

✔ 105°F (40.5°C) or above, go to your veterinarian. This is probably an emergency; 106°F (41°C) or above is dangerous. Try to cool your dog.

✔ 98°F (36.7°C) or below, call your veterinarian for advice. Try to warm your dog.

✔ 96°F (36.5°C) or below, go to your veterinarian. Treat for hypothermia on the way by warming your dog.

Pulse

To check the pulse, cup your hand around the top of your dog's rear leg so your fingers are near the top almost where the leg joins the body. Feel for the pulse in the femoral artery. Normal adult Pekingese pulse rate is 70 to 120 beats per minute.

Hydration

Check hydration by touching the gums, which should be slick, not sticky, or by lifting the skin on the back and letting it go. It should snap back into place quickly, not remain tented. Sticky gums and tented skin indicate dehydration.

Pekingese and Anesthesia

Anesthesia is never taken lightly in any breed, but is even more of a concern in Pekingese. Many procedures that would require anesthesia in more excitable breeds can be done in wide-awake Pekes, but it depends on the individual.

Your veterinarian should be aware of the following anesthesia advice: Pekingese are hard to intubate, and they require a shorter endotracheal tube than might be guessed from their size. They appear to require less anesthesia than other dogs of comparable size. A Pekingese should remain intubated until it is awake, and should spend its recovery on its stomach to lessen the chance its soft palate or large tongue will block the airway. Swelling in the pharynx or larynx, which can occur with intubation, can be very serious.

If your veterinarian is not experienced anesthetizing Pekes or other brachycephalic breeds, ask for a referral to one who is.

Lethargic dogs are often sick dogs.

Healthy Pekes tend to look forward to activities and adventure.

If your dog has been vomiting or has diarrhea, she may instantly lose any water you give her, in which case your veterinarian may need to give your dog fluids under the skin, or better, in a vein.

Common Ailments and Symptoms

Problems of the hair and skin are described on pages 63–65; those of the teeth, ears, and eyes on pages 66–69.

Diarrhea

All dogs get diarrhea, but in Pekingese it is not only a health concern, but a potential grooming nightmare. Diarrhea can result from overexcitement or nervousness, a change in diet or water, sensitivity to certain foods, overeating, intestinal parasites, viral or bacterial infections, or ingestion of toxic substances.

Bloody diarrhea, diarrhea with vomiting, fever, or other signs of toxicity, or diarrhea that lasts for more than a day should not be allowed to continue without veterinary advice. Some of these could be symptomatic of potentially fatal disorders.

Less severe diarrhea can be treated at home by withholding or severely restricting food and water for 24 hours. Ice cubes can be given to satisfy thirst. Administer Immodium in the same weight dosage as recommended for humans. A bland diet consisting of rice, tapioca, or cooked macaroni, along with cottage cheese or tofu for protein, should be given for several days. Feed nothing else. The intestinal tract needs time off in order to heal.

Vomiting

Vomiting is a common occurrence that may or may not indicate a serious problem. You should consult your veterinarian immediately if your dog vomits a foul substance resembling fecal matter (indicating a blockage in the intestinal tract), blood (partially digested blood resembles coffee grounds), or if there is projectile vomiting. Sporadic vomiting with poor appetite and generally poor condition could indicate internal parasites or a more serious internal disease that should also be checked by your veterinarian.

Overeating: Overeating is a common cause of occasional vomiting in puppies, especially if they follow eating with playing. Feed smaller meals more frequently if this becomes a problem. Vomiting after eating grass is common and usually of no great concern. Regurgitation immediately after meals could indicate an obstruction of the esophagus. Repeated vomiting could indicate that the dog has eaten spoiled food, undigestible objects, or may have a stomach illness. Veterinary advice should be sought. Meanwhile, withhold food (or feed as directed for diarrhea), and restrict water.

Coughing

Any persistent cough should be checked by your veterinarian. Coughing irritates the throat and can lead to secondary infections if allowed to continue unchecked. It can also cause swelling of the larynx, possibly interfering with breathing. There are many reasons for coughing, including allergies, foreign bodies, pneumonia, tracheal

The Medical Kit

You should maintain a first aid/medical kit for your Pekingese, which should contain at least:
- rectal thermometer
- scissors
- tweezer
- sterile gauze dressings
- self-adhesive bandage
- instant cold compress
- antidiarrhea medication
- ophthalmic ointment
- soap
- antiseptic skin ointment
- hydrogen peroxide
- clean sponge
- pen light
- syringe
- towel
- stethoscope (optional)
- oxygen (optional)
- first aid instructions
- veterinarian and emergency clinic numbers
- poison control center number

collapse and tumors, but two of the most common are kennel cough and heart disease.

Kennel cough is a highly communicable airborne disease caused by several different infectious agents, but all cause similar symptoms. Vaccinations are available and are an especially good idea if you plan to have your dog around other dogs at training classes or while being boarded.

Heart disease can result in coughing following exercise or in the evening. Treatment with diuretics and specific heart medication(s) prescribed by your veterinarian can help alleviate the coughing for a while.

Urinary Tract Diseases

If your dog has difficulty or pain in urination, urinates suddenly and often, but in small amounts, or passes cloudy or bloody urine, it may be suffering from a problem of the bladder, urethra, or prostate. Your veterinarian will need to examine your Pekingese to determine the exact nature of the problem. Bladder infections must be treated promptly to prevent the infection from reaching the kidneys.

Kidney diseases: Kidney disease, ultimately leading to kidney failure, is one of the most common ailments of older dogs. The earliest symptom is usually increased urination. Although the excessive urination may cause problems in keeping your house clean or your night's sleep intact, *never* try to restrict water from a dog with kidney disease. Increased urination can also be a sign of diabetes or a urinary tract infection. Your veterinarian can determine the cause with some simple tests, and each of these conditions can be treated.

Prostate: In males, infections of the prostate gland can lead to repeated urinary tract infections, and sometimes painful defecation or blood and pus in the urine. Long-term antibiotic therapy and castration is usually the treatment of choice.

Impacted Anal Sacs

Dogs have two anal sacs that are normally emptied by rectal pressure during defecation. Their musky-smelling contents may also be forcibly ejected when a dog is extremely frightened. Sometimes they fail to empty properly and become impacted or infected. This is more common in small dogs, obese dogs, dogs with seborrhea, and dogs that seldom have firm stools. Constant licking of the anus or scooting of the anus along the ground are characteristic signs of anal sac impaction. Not only is this an extremely uncomfortable condition for your dog, but left unattended, the impacted sacs can become abscessed. Your veterinarian can show you how to empty the anal sacs yourself. Some dogs may never need to have their anal sacs expressed, but others may need regular attention. In some instances, these sacs may require surgical removal.

Endocrine Disorders

Hormone-related disorders in the dog include diabetes, hypothyroidism, and Cushing's syndrome. The most common is hypothyroidism; its signs are often subtle, but may include weight gain, lethargy, and coat problems such as oiliness, dullness, symmetrical hair loss, and hair that is easily pulled out.

The symptoms of diabetes include increased drinking and urination, and sometimes increased appetite with weight loss.

Cushing's syndrome (hyperadrenocorticism) is seen mostly in older dogs, and is characterized by increased drinking and urination, a pot-bellied appearance, symmetrical hair loss on the body, and hyperpigmentation of the skin. This condition is often accompanied by infections because Cushing's dogs have diminished immunity to infection.

All of these conditions can be diagnosed with simple tests, and can be effectively treated with drugs.

Limping

Puppies are especially susceptible to bone and joint injuries, and should never be allowed to jump from high places or run until exhausted. Persistent limping in puppies may result from one of several developmental bone problems, and should be professionally evaluated. Both puppies and adults should be kept off slippery floors that could cause them to lose their footing. Clipping the long hair that covers the foot pads can also help prevent your Peke from slipping.

Limping may or may not indicate a serious problem. When associated with extreme pain, fever, swelling, deformity, or grinding or popping sounds, you should have your veterinarian examine your Pekingese at once. Ice packs may help minimize swelling if applied immediately after an injury. Mild lameness should be treated by complete rest; if it still persists after three days, your dog will need to be examined by her veterinarian.

Knee injuries are common in dogs; most do not get well on their own. Avoid pain medications that might encourage the use of an injured limb.

In older dogs, or dogs with a previous injury, limping is often the result of osteoarthritis. Arthritis can be treated with aspirin, but should be done so only under veterinary supervision. Do not use ibuprofen or naxopren.

Nerve damage: Lameness in which the leg appears paralyzed, or when the dog places the top of the foot on the ground, could be due to nerve damage. One of the more common types of rear end paralysis in Pekes results from herniated intervertebral discs, which may or may not respond to surgical treatment. The possibility of herniated discs can be lessened by not allowing your Peke to jump off furniture or high places or to go up or down stairs.

Brachycephalic Syndrome

Dogs with flat faces tend to have compacted respiratory systems, which leads to a condition

called brachycephalic syndrome. It consists of a group of anatomical abnormalities including elongated soft palate, stenotic nares, and sometimes other abnormalities that cause breathing problems.

The soft palate is the mobile flap that extends from the rear of the roof of the mouth. Its purpose is to prevent food and water from going into the nasal passages when swallowing. When elongated, it hangs in the airway or larynx during inhalation, obstructing the airway. An affected dog may have to breathe through the mouth, and may snore, snort, and gag, especially when the dog is hot or excited. The harder the dog breathes, the more the soft palate swells, and the greater the obstruction. Definite diagnosis may need to be made under anesthesia, at which time surgical correction is advised.

Stenotic nares, or constricted nostrils, are the result of overly soft cartilage that forms the

Brachycephalic syndrome, referring to breathing problems created by flat faces and compacted respiratory systems, is the breed's overall biggest health concern.

nostrils. When the dog inhales, the nostrils collapse on themselves, shutting off the air flow. The dog may have labored breathing, mouth breathing, snorting, and a watery or foamy nasal discharge. She may develop a flattened chest and be in generally poor condition. Surgical treatment in which the nostrils are enlarged should be performed as soon as possible in such dogs.

Other components of brachycephalic syndrome may include tortuous turbinates, in which the pathways of the nasal airways are abnormally twisted, and a hypoplastic trachea, in which the trachea is abnormally narrow. Together or separately, these traits cause

breathing difficulties. In turn, the increased suction required to pull air through the obstructed airway sucks the laryngeal walls and saccules (small sacs lining the larynx) into the glottis, and the increased turbulence causes the laryngeal membranes to swell. These cause further airway obstruction.

Adding to the problem, some brachycephalic dogs have underdeveloped tracheal cartilage. Increased sucking forces can contribute to the collapse of the cartilage rings that form the trachea, flattening the trachea and dangerously obstructing air flow. This causes a goose-honk kind of cough, especially when excited; in severe cases the dog shows signs of lack of oxygen.

Note: Airway obstruction creates a vicious circle in which obstruction leads to changes that cause even greater obstruction. Sometimes the condition gets gradually worse without the owner's notice, until something—exercise, hot weather, respiratory infection—causes just enough additional swelling that the trachea totally collapses or the laryngeal saccules or soft palate totally plug the airway, and the dog asphyxiates and dies. If you suspect your Peke has any component of brachycephalic syndrome, don't let it go unchecked until it's spiraled out of control. If possible, have your dog evaluated and treated by a veterinarian experienced with surgical correction of these problems.

Patellar Luxation

Pekingese, like most small dogs, have some predisposition to be affected by patellar luxation, in which the kneecap (patella) slips out of position. When the knee flexes, the patella normally glides along the trochlear groove of the femur, held within the groove by the quadriceps muscle and joint capsule. In some Pekes the groove is too shallow, or the quadriceps' rotational pull is too strong, allowing the patella to ride over the groove's ridge when the knee is flexed. Only by straightening the knee will the patella go back into place. Affected dogs will often take several steps with a hind leg held straight toward the front until the patella pops back into place. It may hurt when it does, so the dog may yelp. In more severe cases, the luxated patella can't pop back on its own. Each time it goes in and out of the groove it wears down the groove's edge, which in turn can cause arthritic changes.

Treatment depends on severity.

✔ For Grade 1, in which the patella seldom pops out of place on its own, and the dog may hold her leg up for a step or two, no treatment is suggested.

✔ For Grade 2, in which the dog often holds her leg up when walking or running, and in which the patella may not pop back in on its own, treatment is seldom suggested.

✔ For Grade 3, in which the dog seldom uses the affected leg, and the patella is permanently out of position, surgery may be suggested.

✔ For Grade 4, in which the dog never uses the affected leg and the patella can't be replaced even manually, surgery is usually suggested.

Patellar luxation is thought to have a strong hereditary basis, probably, like hip dysplasia, inherited in a polygenic fashion. The OFA offers a registry of Pekes that have been checked for patellar luxation, but few Pekingese owners have submitted results.

Medications

Don't give your dog human medications unless you have been directed to do so by your veterinarian. Some medications for humans have no effect on dogs, and some can have a very detrimental effect.

When giving pills, open your dog's mouth and place the pill well to the back and in the middle of the tongue. Close the mouth and gently stroke the throat until your dog swallows. Pre-wetting capsules or covering them with cream cheese or some other food helps prevent capsules from sticking to the tongue or roof of the mouth.

For liquid medicine, tilt the head back and place the liquid in the pouch of the cheek.

Then close your dog's mouth until she swallows. Always give the full course of medications prescribed by your veterinarian.

The Pekingese Pensioner

When is a Pekingese geriatric? It varies among dogs, but most small dogs are described as geriatric at 10 to 12 years of age. In a 1960 study of 158 Pekingese, 80 percent of Pekes that reached adulthood lived to be at least five years of age, 62 percent were alive at 10 years, 36 percent reached their fourteenth year, but none of these survived another year.

As your Peke ages, you may first notice that she sleeps longer and more soundly than she

For many people, the older Pekingese is the most gracious, stately, and beautiful of all.

did as a youngster. Upon awakening, she is slower to get going and may be stiff at first. She may be less eager to play and more content to lie in the sun. Some dogs become cranky and less patient, especially when dealing with puppies or boisterous children. But don't just excuse behavioral changes, especially if sudden, as due simply to aging. They could be symptoms of pain or disease.

Hearing: Older dogs may seem to ignore their owner's commands, but this may be the result of hearing loss. Take care not to startle a dog with impaired hearing, as a startled dog could snap in self-defense.

Eyes: The slight haziness that appears in the older dog's pupils is normal and has minimal effect upon vision, but some dogs, especially those with diabetes, may develop cataracts. These can be removed by a veterinary ophthalmologist if they are severe. Decreased tear production increases the chances of KCS (dry eye) in older Pekes (see page 69). Dogs with gradual vision loss can cope well as long as they are kept in familiar surroundings. Don't rearrange furniture, close usually open doors, or come upon a blind Peke without first speaking. Use baby gates at the head of stairs or edges of decks.

Arthritis: This is a common cause of intermittent lameness. A soft warm bed combined with moderate activity can help, and your veterinarian can prescribe drugs for severe cases.

In some Pekes, the intervertebral discs gradually become displaced and exert pressure on the spinal cord, causing paralysis of the hind legs. The sooner an affected dog is treated, the better the chance of recovery. Surgery is not

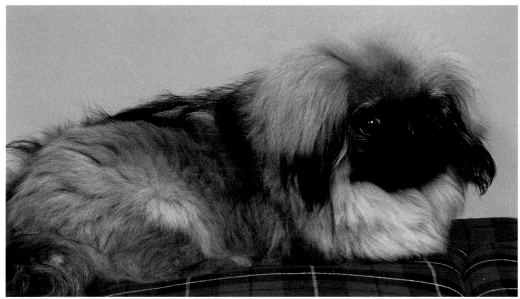

All Pekes appreciate a soft bed, but it's essential for older and sick Pekes.

always successful, and the dog may need special care for the rest of her life. Carts are available that cradle the dog's pelvis and enable the dog to roll merrily along.

Feeding the Older Dog

Older dogs should be fed several small meals instead of one large meal, and should be fed on time. Moistening dry food or feeding canned food can help a dog with tooth loss enjoy her meal.

Although many geriatric dogs are overweight, others lose weight and may need to eat puppy food in order to keep the weight on. But most older dogs do not require a special diet unless they have a particular medical need for it (such as, obesity: low calorie; kidney failure: low phosphorus; heart failure: low sodium). Dogs with these problems may require special prescription dog foods that better address their needs.

Skin Care

Like people, dogs lose skin moisture as they age, and though dogs don't wrinkle, their skin can become dry and itchy as a result. Regular brushing can stimulate oil production. Older dogs tend to have a stronger body odor, but don't just ignore increased odors. They could indicate specific problems, such as periodontal disease, impacted anal sacs, seborrhea, ear infections, or even kidney disease. Any strong odor should be checked by your veterinarian.

Health Risks

There is evidence that the immune system may be less effective in older dogs. This means that it is increasingly important to shield your dog from infectious disease, chilling, overheating, and any stressful conditions. Older dogs present a somewhat greater anesthesia risk.

Most of this increased risk can be negated, however, by first screening dogs with a complete medical workup.

The older dog should be seen by its veterinarian at least biyearly. Blood tests can detect early stages of disease that can benefit from treatment. The owner must take responsibility for observing any health changes. Some of the more common changes, along with some of the more common conditions they may indicate in older dogs, are:

✔ Limping: arthritis, patellar luxation
✔ Nasal discharge: tumor, periodontal disease
✔ Coughing: heart disease, tracheal collapse, lung cancer
✔ Difficulty eating: periodontal disease, oral tumors
✔ Decreased appetite: kidney, liver, or heart disease, pancreatitis, cancer
✔ Increased appetite: diabetes, Cushing's syndrome
✔ Weight loss: heart, liver, or kidney disease, diabetes, cancer
✔ Abdominal distension: heart or kidney disease, Cushing's syndrome, tumor
✔ Increased urination: diabetes, kidney, or liver disease, cystitis, Cushing's syndrome
✔ Diarrhea: kidney or liver disease, pancreatitis

The above list is by no means inclusive of all symptoms or problems they may indicate. Vomiting and diarrhea can signal many different problems; keep in mind that a small older dog cannot tolerate the dehydration that results from continued vomiting or diarrhea and you should not let it continue unchecked.

In general, any ailment that an older dog has is magnified in severity compared to the same symptoms in a younger dog. This is especially true of any problems with breathing or over-heating in the Peke. Don't be lulled into a false sense of security just because you own a Pekingese. A long life depends upon good genes, good care, and good luck.

If you are lucky enough to have an old Pekingese, you still must accept that an end will come. Heart disease, kidney failure, and cancer eventually claim most of these senior citizens. Early detection can help delay their effects, but unfortunately, can seldom prevent them ultimately.

To Breed or Not to Breed

You may be tempted to breed your Pekingese, but consider these caveats first:

Dystocia and Caesarean Sections

Brachycephalic breeds, breeds with large forequarters and narrow hindquarters, and small breeds in general have a greater tendency to have *dystocia*, the difficulty or inability to deliver a puppy through the birth canal. Pekingese are prone to dystocia, and often require cesarean sections (C-sections) to save the lives of the puppies and dam.

Many experienced Peke breeders elect to have a C-section performed for every litter. In this way the dam is not already in trouble before undergoing surgery, and arrangements can be made for surgery during regular office hours.

Eclampsia

Eclampsia is a life-threatening convulsive condition that may occur in late pregnancy or more commonly, during lactation. It is more prevalent in small breeds and with larger litters.

The condition is brought about by a depletion of calcium. Prenatal supplementation may

That dogs live their lives in dog years makes sharing them difficult for those of us who live our lives in human years. Yet each Peke manages to be the dog of a lifetime.

actually promote eclampsia by interfering with the internal calcium-regulating mechanisms.

Once eclampsia does occur, the bitch must be taken immediately to the veterinarian for an injection of calcium and Vitamin D in order to save her life. Calcium may be given by mouth if she can swallow and if the trip to the veterinarian is long, but even then may not be absorbed enough to help much. *Eclampsia is an extreme emergency.*

Know the phone number and location of the emergency veterinarian in your area.

Deciding whether or not you have an emergency can sometimes be difficult. What would not be an emergency for the average dog may very well be an emergency for a Peke. The following situations are all emergencies. **For all cases, administer the first aid treatment outlined and seek the nearest veterinary help immediately.** Call the clinic first so that they can prepare.

In General

✔ Make sure breathing passages are open. Remove any collar and check the mouth and throat.

✔ Be calm and reassuring. A calm dog is less likely to go into shock.

✔ Move the dog as little and as gently as possible.

Shock

Signs: Very pale gums, weakness, unresponsiveness, faint pulse, shivering.

Treatment: Keep the dog warm and calm; control any bleeding; check breathing, pulse, and consciousness, and treat these problems if needed.

Heatstroke

Signs: Rapid, loud breathing; abundant thick saliva, bright red mucous membranes, high rectal temperature. Later signs: unsteadiness, diarrhea, coma.

Treatment: Immediately immerse the dog in cool (not ice) water and then place it in front of a fan. You must lower your dog's body temperature quickly (but do not lower it below 100°F [37.8°C]). If your dog has been shaved, cover him with a cold wet towel and place him in front of a fan.

Breathing Difficulties

Signs: Gasping for breath with head extended, anxiety, weakness; advances to loss of consciousness, bluish tongue (exception: carbon monoxide poisoning causes a bright red tongue).

Treatment: If not breathing, give mouth-to-nose respiration:

1. Open dog's mouth, clear passage of secretions and foreign bodies.

2. Pull dog's tongue forward.

3. Seal your mouth over dog's nose and mouth; blow gently into dog's nose for three seconds, then release.

4. Continue until dog breathes on its own.

If due to **drowning,** turn dog upside down, holding it by the hind legs, so that water can run out of its mouth. Then administer mouth-to-nose respiration, with the dog's head positioned lower than its lungs.

For **obstructions,** wrap your hands around the abdomen, behind the rib cage, and compress briskly. Repeat if needed. If the dog loses consciousness, extend the head and neck forward, pull the tongue out

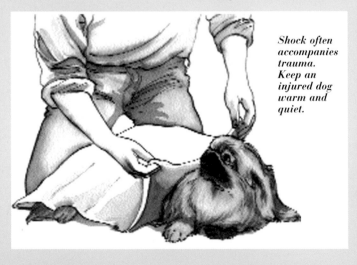

Shock often accompanies trauma. Keep an injured dog warm and quiet.

fully, and explore the throat for any foreign objects.

Poisoning

Signs: Varies according to poison, but commonly include vomiting, convulsions, staggering, collapse.

Treatment: Call the veterinarian or poison control hotline at once and give as much information as possible. Induce vomiting (except in the cases outlined below) by giving either hydrogen peroxide (mixed 1:1 with water), salt water, or dry mustard and water. Treat for shock and get to the veterinarian immediately. Be prepared for convulsions or respiratory distress.

Do *not* induce vomiting if the poison was an acid, alkali, petroleum product, solvent, cleaner, tranquilizer, or if a sharp object was swallowed; also do *not* induce vomiting if the dog is severely depressed, convulsing, comatose, or if more than two hours have passed since ingestion.

If the dog is not convulsing or unconscious: dilute the poison by giving milk, vegetable oil, or egg whites. Activated charcoal can adsorb many toxins. Baking soda or milk of magnesia can be given for ingested acids, and vinegar or lemon juice for ingested alkalis.

Two of the most common and life-threatening poisons eaten by dogs are Warfarin (rodent poison) and ethylene glycol (antifreeze). Veterinary treatment must be obtained within two to four hours of ingestion of even tiny amounts if the dog's life is to be saved.

Convulsions

Signs: Drooling, stiffness, muscle spasms.

Treatment: Wrap the dog securely in a blanket to prevent him from injuring himself on the furniture or stairs. Remove other dogs from the area. *Never* put your hands in a convulsing dog's mouth. Treat for shock. Make note of all characteristics and sequences of seizure activity, which can help to diagnose the cause.

Open Wounds

Signs: Consider wounds to be an emergency if there is profuse bleeding, if extremely deep, or if open to chest cavity, abdominal cavity, or head.

Treatment: Control massive bleeding first. Cover the wound with clean dressing and apply pressure; apply more dressings over the others until bleeding stops. Also, elevate wound site, and apply cold pack to site. If an extremity, apply pressure to the closest pressure point as follows:
• For a front leg: inside of front leg just above the elbow
• For a rear leg: inside of the thigh where the femoral artery crosses the thighbone
• For the tail: underside of the tail close to where it joins the body.

Transport to a veterinarian immediately.

Use a tourniquet only in life-threatening situations and when all other attempts have failed. Check for signs of shock.

Sucking chest wounds: Place a sheet of plastic or other nonporous material over the hole and bandage it to make as airtight a seal as possible.

Abdominal wounds: Place a warm wet sterile dressing over any protruding internal organs; cover with a bandage or towel. Do not attempt to push organs back into the dog.

Head wounds: Apply gentle pressure to control bleeding. Monitor for loss of consciousness or shock and treat accordingly.

Again, the procedures outlined above are first aid only. They do not take the place of the emergency veterinary clinic. Nor is the above list a complete catalog of emergency situations. Situations not described can usually be treated with the same first aid as for humans.

THE PROUDEST PEKINGESE

Any Pekingese owner knows the most fulfilling times with their dogs are the times spent snuggling in front of the television, playing in the den, or exploring the neighborhood. Even so, you can have even more adventures if you decide to enter the world of canine competitions.

Pekes on Parade

The Pekingese has been one of the most consistently popular show dogs in history. Amidst the barking, tail-wagging dogs dancing for bits of liver, the Pekingese stands out as above it all. While other breeds race around the ring, the Peke strolls leisurely with the attitude that the show will just have to wait until he has taken his sweet time getting around the ring. Pekingese quality is so consistently high that competition can be extremely tough, so if you think you might want to try showing, be careful to take your time choosing the very best dog available. If you plan to breed your Pekingese, you should plan to compete in conformation in

All Pekingese are proud, but those that get to prove it also make their people proud.

order to demonstrate to others that your dog is as perfect as you know he is.

Show Ring Greats

At the end of a dog show, one dog alone among the thousands competing stands undefeated—the Best in Show (BIS) winner. To win one such award is a coveted and remarkable achievement. Ch. Chik T'Sun of Caversham won more than 100 Best in Shows, and held the record for many years for the top winning BIS dog of any breed in America. Among his supreme awards was the ultimate: BIS at Westminster, America's most prestigious dog event. Remarkably, two other Pekes have also won this highest honor in dogdom: Ch. St. Aubrey Dragonora of Elsdon and Ch. Wendessa Crown Prince.

The toy group at Westminster has been won by a Pekingese 23 times—more than any other toy breed.

The Peke of Perfection

Weight and size: The Pekingese standard covers small details as well as overall appearance. It calls for a compact dog with a heavy front and lighter hindquarters, with head large in proportion to its body. It has a stocky muscular body, and is surprisingly heavy for its size. However, it must not weigh more than 14 pounds (6.4 kg), although all weights under that are equally correct.

It is slightly longer than tall when measured from the forechest to the buttocks. The overall outline is an approximate ratio of 3 high to 5 long.

Pekingese are among the most competitive of all breeds at dog shows.

Personality: Overall, its image is lionlike, implying courage, dignity, boldness, and self-esteem rather than daintiness or delicacy. Its temperament is one of directness, independence and individuality. Its combination of regal dignity, intelligence, and self-importance make for a good-natured, opinionated, and affectionate companion to those who have earned its respect.

Coat: The coat is long, coarse-textured, straight, and stand-off, with a thick, soft under-coat. It is noticeably longer on the neck and shoulder area, forming a mane. Although a long, profuse coat is desirable, it should not obscure the shape of the body. Long feathering is found on the toes, backs of the thighs and forelegs, with longer fringing on the ears and tail. There should be no obvious trimming or sculpting.

Color, markings, and the presence or absence of a black mask are immaterial; however, the exposed skin of the muzzle, nose, lips and eye rims should be black.

Gait: The gait is unhurried, dignified, free, and strong, with a slight roll over the shoulders. This motion is smooth and effortless and is as free as possible from bouncing, prancing, or jarring. The rolling gait results from a combination of the bowed forelegs, well-laid back shoulders, full broad chest, and narrow light rear, all of which produce adequate reach and moderate drive.

Highlights of the Standard
- Massive, broad, flat topskull
- Wide-set eyes, cheekbones
- Broad lower jaw
- Skull is wider than deep.

- Rectangular, envelope-shaped appearance of the head
- A line drawn horizontally over the top of the nose intersects slightly above the center of the eyes.
- Flat facial profile, with chin, nose leather, and brow in one plane that slants slightly backward from chin to forehead.
- Heart-shaped ears, set on the front corners of the topskull, and lying flat against the head. Ear leather does not extend below the jaw. Long, heavy fringing frames the sides of the face.
- Large, dark, round, eyes; bold but not bulging. The white of the eye does not show when the dog is looking straight ahead.
- Broad, short, black nose
- Wide, open nostrils
- Wrinkle extends from one cheek over the bridge of the nose in a wide inverted V, obscuring stop. Not so heavy as to crowd the facial features, obscure more than a small portion of the eyes, or fall forward over any portion of the nose leather.
- Flat, broad muzzle, well-filled-in below the eyes.
- Whiskers add to the desired expression.
- Lower jaw is undershot and broad. Neither teeth nor tongue show when the mouth is closed.
- Lips black and close-fitting.
- Short, thick neck.
- Pear-shaped, compact body, low to the ground. Heavy in front with well-sprung ribs slung between the forelegs.
- Broad, full forechest without a protruding breastbone.
- Underline rises from the deep chest to the lighter loin, thus forming a narrow waist.
- Straight topline.
- Short loin.
- High-set tail, slightly arched and carried well over the back, free of kinks or curls. Long, profuse, straight fringing may fall to either side.
- Short, thick, heavy-boned forelegs, moderately bowed between the pastern and elbow.
- Well-laid-back shoulders fitting smoothly onto the body.
- Elbows close to the body.
- Front feet turned out slightly when standing or moving.
- Gently sloping pasterns.
- Hindquarters are lighter in bone than the forequarters.
- Moderate angulation of stifle and hock.
- When viewed from behind, the rear legs are reasonably close and parallel, and the feet point straight ahead.

Disqualification: Weight over 14 pounds (6.4 kg).

The face has an envelope shape.

The show dog must have a perfectly groomed coat.

The Heeling Pekingese

If your Peke is more than just another pretty face, you may wish to enter an obedience trial, where your little genius can earn degrees attesting to his mastery of various levels of obedience. You and your dog will have to prove yourselves in front of a judge at three different obedience trials in order to officially have an obedience title become part of your dog's name.

Plan on training your Pekingese the commands *"heel," "sit," "down," "come,"* and *"stay"* for use in everyday life. Add the *"stand for exam,"* and your dog will have the basic skills necessary to earn the AKC Companion Dog (CD) title.

Higher Degrees

Higher degrees of Companion Dog Excellent (CDX) or Utility Dog (UD) and Utility Dog Excellent (UDX) also require retrieving, jumping, hand signals, and scent discrimination. The OTCH degree is an Obedience Trial Champion; these are given only to dogs with UDs that outscore many other UD dogs in many, many trials.

If you are at an obedience trial and see that an OTCH dog of any breed is entered, take the time to watch it go through its paces. The first OTCH Pekingese earned the title in 1995—OTCH Gidget to the Rescue, a Peke that was rescued from an animal shelter.

Rally!

If obedience competition sounds a little intimidating, fear not! Rally obedience is a more free-form obedience competition in which you and your dog complete a course with signs telling you what to do at each station. You can give multiple commands and praise your dog throughout—more like you would do in real life!

Agile Pekes

Agility is basically an obstacle course for dogs. The standard course obstacles include various jumps, open and closed tunnels, weave poles, a pause table, a teeter, a tall A-frame, and elevated balance beam. The jumps can be single bars, double bars, broad, solid, and even a tire.

An alternative course type, called Jumpers With Weaves (JWW), uses just the jumps, tunnels, and weaves. If the jumps seem too high for your dog, you can elect to compete in the Preferred class, which has lower jump heights.

The Good Pekingese Citizen

In order to formally recognize dogs that behave in public, the AKC offers the Canine Good Citizen (CGC) certificate. To earn this title your Pekingese must pass the following exercises:
- Accepting a friendly stranger who greets you
- Sitting politely for petting by a stranger
- Allowing a stranger to pet and groom it
- Walking politely on a loose lead
- Walking through a crowd on a lead
- Sitting and lying down on command and staying in place while on a 20-foot (6.1 m) line
- Reacting politely to another dog
- Reacting calmly to distractions
- Remaining calm when held three minutes in the owner's absence.

The Healing Pekingese

Studies have shown that pet ownership increases life expectancy, and petting animals can lower blood pressure. In recent years, nursing home residents have come to look forward to visits by dogs, including Pekingese. These dogs must be meticulously well mannered and well groomed; to be registered as a Certified Therapy Dog, a dog must demonstrate that it will act in an obedient, outgoing, gentle manner to strangers. The eye-catching Peke, with its calm personality and small size, is a natural for people who may not appreciate being overwhelmed by a licking clown. A friendly Peke could make a big difference in a lonely person's day.

Pekingese combine elegance and playfulness, making many of them ideal as therapy dogs.

■INFORMATION

Organizations
The American Kennel Club
260 Madison Avenue
New York, NY 10016
(212) 696-8200
www.akc.org

AKC Registration
5580 Centerview Drive
Raleigh, NC 27606
(919) 233-9767

The Pekingese Club of America
(address changes periodically)
Diane Renihan, Secretary
(561) 743-0888
www.pekingeseclub.org

The Pekingese Club of America Breeder Referral
Edwin B. Doroliat
799 Widgeon Street
Foster City, CA 94404-1355
(415) 505-8901
E-mail: conquette@aol.com

Pekingese Rescue
(address changes periodically)
I. Louis Harden, Chairperson
Pasadena, MD
(410) 255-2166

Orthopedic Foundation for Animals
2300 Nifong Boulevard
Columbia, MO 65201
(314) 442-0418
www.offa.org

Home Again Microchip Service
1-800-LONELY-ONE

Magazines
The Orient Express
8848 Beverly Hills
Lakeland, FL 33809-1604
(941) 858-3839
www.dmcg.com

Several all-breed magazines are listed at
www.dogchannel.com

Books
Coile, Caroline. *Congratulations! It's a Dog.*
Hauppauge, NY: Barron's Educational Series,
Inc., 2005.
———. *Encyclopedia of Dogs Breeds.* Hauppauge,
NY: Barron's Educational Series, Inc., 2005.

━━━━ **TIP** ━━━━

Internet Information
You can find information about all-breed
dog shows from the America Kennel Club
www.akc.org. Click on Events, then Conformation, then Events and Awards Search,
then Search Events; or click on Events,
Conformation, then Superintendents, and
then search for the superintendent that
organizes shows in your region of the
country. A popular superintendent site is
www.infodog.com.
You can also find information about local
dog clubs from the AKC Web site. Click on
Clubs, then Club Search, then Conformation,
then your state, then Search.

Web Sites

Canine Health Foundation	*www.akcchf.org*
Kennel Cubs Worldwide	*http://henceforths.com/kennel_clubs.html*
The Pekingese Club (UK)	*www.thepekingeseclub.co.uk*
The Pekingese Webring	*www.dropbears.com/p/pekingese/*
Therapy Dogs International	*www.tdi-dog.org*
Todd's Pekingese Pages	*www.biske.com/peke/*
Westminster Kennel Club	*www.westminsterkennelclub.org*

The Pekingese "must suggest its Chinese origin in its directness, independence, individuality, and expression. Its image is lionlike." From the AKC standard.

———. *Show Me! A Dog Showing Primer.* Hauppauge, NY: Barron's Educational Series, Inc., 1997.

Denlinger, Milo. *The Complete Pekingese.* Silver Spring: Denlinger's, 1957.

Godden, Rumer. *The Butterfly Lions: The Story of the Pekingese in History, Legend, and Art.* New York: Viking Press, 1978.

Hill, Herminie Warner. *Pekingese.* London: Foyle, 1970.

Quigley, Dorothy. *The Quigley Book of the Pekingese.* New York: Howell, 1964.

Stannard, Liz. *The Complete Pekingese.* New York: Howell, 1999.

Williams, Vandella, and Adele Summers. *Pekingese.* Wiltshire, UK: Crowood Press, 1990.

Videos

Pekingese Standard: *www.akc.org/store/*

■INDEX

About the Authors

Caroline Coile is an award-winning author who has written articles about dogs for both scientific and lay publications. She holds a Ph.D. in the field of neuroscience and behavior, with special interests in canine sensory systems, genetics, and behavior. Her own dogs have been nationally ranked in conformation, obedience, and field-trial competition.

Photo Credits

Norvia Behling: pages 17 (top), 18, 30, 42, 44, 46, 48, 65, 91; Kent Dannen: pages 8, 9, 17 (bottom), 20, 22, 34, 39, 61, 63, 67, 78, 83, 89; Tara Darling: pages 4, 6, 7, 8, 21, 22, 37, 38, 45, 53, 54, 86, 88, 93; Isabelle Francais: pages 2–3, 5, 10, 11, 12, 15 (top and bottom), 16, 23, 24, 25, 26, 28, 31, 33, 35, 36, 40, 43, 50, 58, 59, 60, 62, 68, 70, 71, 73, 74, 80, 81, 87, 90; Pets by Paulette: pages 13, 19, 32, 48, 49.

Important Note

This pet owner's guide tells the reader how to buy and care for a Pekingese. The author and the publisher consider it important to point out that the advice given in the book is meant primarily for normally developed puppies from a good breeder—that is, dogs of excellent physical health and good character.

Anyone who adopts a fully grown dog should be aware that the animal has already formed its basic impressions of human beings. The new owner should watch the animal carefully, including its behavior toward humans, and should meet the previous owner. If the dog comes from a shelter, it may be possible to get some information on the dog's background and peculiarities there. There are dogs that, as a result of bad experiences with humans, behave in an unnatural manner or may even bite. Only people that have experience with dogs should take in such animals.

Caution is further advised in the association of children with dogs, in meeting with other dogs, and in exercising the dog without a leash.

Even well-behaved and carefully supervised dogs sometimes do damage to someone else's property or cause accidents. It is therefore in the owner's interest to be adequately insured against such eventualities, and we strongly urge all dog owners to purchase a liability policy that covers their dog.

Cover Photos

Isabelle Francais: front cover, inside front cover, back cover, and inside back cover.

All inquiries should be addressed to:
Barron's Educational Series, Inc.
250 Wireless Boulevard
Hauppauge, NY 11788
www.barronseduc.com

ISBN-13: 978-0-7641-3401-2
ISBN-10: 0-7641-3401-9

Library of Congress Catalog Card No. 2006042957

Library of Congress Cataloging-in-Publication Data
Coile, D. Caroline.
    Pekingese : everything about purchase, care, nutrition, behavior, and training / D. Caroline Coile ; illustrations by Michele Earle-Bridges.
        p. cm. — (A complete pet owner's manual)
    Includes bibliographical references (p.   ) and index.
    ISBN-13: 978-0-7641-3401-2
    ISBN-10: 0-7641-3401-9
    1. Pekingese dog. I. Earle-Bridges, Michele. II. Title. III. Series.

SF429.P3C58   2006
636.76—dc22   2006042957

Printed in China
9 8 7 6 5 4 3 2 1